Whistler Landscapes and Seascapes

Whistler Landscapes and Seascapes

BY DONALD HOLDEN

Watson-Guptill Publications, New York,

in cooperation with the Freer Gallery of Art,

Smithsonian Institution, Washington, D.C.

First published 1969 by Watson-Guptill Publications,
165 West 46 Street, New York, New York 10036, U.S.A.

Manufactured in Japan.

Library of Congress Catalog Card Number: 70-76573

For Blake, who says museums are tough,
for Wendy, who says that paintings are neat,
and for Willi, who listens.

We often owe great debts to creditors who have forgotten that they ever made the loan. So it is with me. The text of this book approaches painting by a route suggested by Mark Van Doren, who once said to a class at Columbia, "Perhaps the best way to understand a poem is to imagine it still unwritten." Robert Beverly Hale drove this lesson home at the Art Students League, where he taught his anatomy class that a drawing is, above all, a pattern of decisions. Theodoros Stamos unwittingly suggested this book nearly twenty years ago when Whistler was no more than a name to me: "You know who really has magic? Whistler." And I wonder if this book would have been written at all without Roland Wojciechowsky, who called faithfully each Saturday morning to take an awestruck little boy to museums.

My co-workers at Watson-Guptill Publications—Jules Perel, Susan Meyer (who edited the text), Marilynn Koch, Sally Saunders, James Craig (who designed the book), Judith Levy, Gisela Moriarty, Margit Malmstrom (who assembled the illustrations), and Candy Nathanson (who told callers that Mr. Holden was in Outer Mongolia and could not be reached)—encouraged me to walk out of the office, slam the door, and get the writing done. My warmest thanks to them for cheering me on.

The major illustrated books on Whistler are nearly all of British origin; thus, color plates of Whistlers in British collections are well represented in the available literature. For this reason, the color plates in this volume are drawn entirely from American collections. This was also necessary for technical reasons, since most of the paintings have never been reproduced in color and were specially photographed under the publisher's supervision.

By far the most comprehensive Whistler collection in America is in Washington's superb Freer Gallery of Art, whose pictures are almost unknown to the public because the terms of the Freer bequest forbid the collection to travel. The gallery is particularly rich in the small, late oils and watercolors which are so rarely reproduced and which appear, many of them actual size, in the pages that follow. By virtue of quality and sheer numbers, it is inevitable that the Freer collection dominates this book. I am indebted to John A. Pope, Director; Harold P. Stern, Assistant Director; Raymond A. Schwartz, Chief of the Freer Photographic Laboratory; and Martin Amt, Museum Specialist, for their cooperation.

Museums which generously made paintings available for reproduction are:

Art Institute of Chicago
Detroit Institute of Arts
Fogg Art Museum
Freer Gallery of Art
Hill-Stead Museum
Isabella Stewart Gardner Museum
John G. Johnson Collection
Museum of Fine Arts, Boston
National Gallery of Art
New Britain Museum of American Art
Thomas Gilcrease Institute
Wadsworth Atheneum

My special thanks to Andrew McLaren Young of the University of Glasgow, who permitted me to condense the excellent chronology of Whistler's life in the catalog of the Whistler exhibition which Mr. Young organized in 1960 for The Arts Council of Great Britain and the English Speaking Union of the United States; he was also kind enough to check the condensation before it went to press.

Color Plates

Condensed from Andrew McLaren Young's catalog of the 1960 Whistler exhibition in London and New York (see bibliographical note).

1834   Born Lowell, Massachusetts, July 11. Father: Major George Washington Whistler, civil engineer. Mother: Anna Matilda McNeill.

1843   Family moved to Russia, where father worked on railroad.

1845   Took drawing lessons, Imperial Academy of Science, St. Petersburg; also private drawing lessons.

1848   Attended school in England, where his half sister, Deborah, had married Dr. Francis Seymour Haden, later well known as an etcher.

1849   Family returned to America on father's death; lived at Pomfret, Connecticut.

1851   Entered U. S. Military Academy, West Point. Added McNeill, mother's maiden name, to his own.

1854   Discharged from West Point for deficiency in chemistry; top of class in drawing. Joined drawing division, U. S. Coast Geodetic Survey; etched maps, topographical plans.

1855   Decided to become an artist. Moved to Paris. Attended Ecole Impériale et Spéciale de Dessin.

1856   Attended Académie Gleyre.

1857   Saw fourteen paintings by or attributed to Velazquez at Art Treasures Exhibition, Manchester.

1858   Produced etchings, "French Set." Met Fantin-Latour. This led to later meetings with Legros, Carolus-Duran, Bracquemond, Courbet.

1859   First important painting, *At the Piano*, rejected at Salon, but exhibited at Bonvin's studio, praised by Courbet. Moved to London. Began series of etchings, "Thames Set."

1860   *At the Piano* exhibited at Royal Academy, praised by Millais. Joanna Heffernan became mistress, principal model.

1861   Met Manet in Paris. Painted first major seascape, *The Coast of Brittany*.

1862   *The White Girl* (afterwards entitled *Symphony in White, No. 1*) rejected by R. A., but *The Coast of Brittany* and *The Thames in Ice* accepted, well received. Met D. G. Rossetti. Thames etchings exhibited in Paris, praised by Baudelaire.

1863   Met Swinburne, Morris, Burne-Jones. *The White Girl* rejected at Salon, but one of chief talking-points at Salon des Refusés. Etchings won gold medal at The Hague.

1864   Began painting oriental subjects. *The Lange Lijzen* and *Wapping* well received at R. A.

1865   *The Little White Girl*, other pictures, shown at R. A. Joined Courbet at Trouville, where Monet and Daubigny were also painting. Met Albert Moore; both painted classically draped figures.

1866   Visited South America; painted seascapes in Valparaiso. Parted from Jo.

1867   Exhibited in smaller London dealers' exhibitions, Salon, R. A. Rejected Courbet's realism. Produced no finished paintings until 1870, but experimented with classically draped figures in Japanese setting.

1871   Published "Thames Set" etchings. Began Thames nocturnes.

1872   *The Artist's Mother* grudgingly admitted to R. A. This was last picture he ever submitted. From this time onwards, began to give nearly all pictures titles analogous to musical compositions. Began to paint commissioned portraits.

1874   First one man exhibition, Flemish Gallery, London. Etchings exhibited, Liverpool Art Club. Maud Franklin, later his mistress, began to appear as model.

1875   Most controversial picture, *The Falling Rocket*, exhibited at French Gallery, London.

1877   Completed decoration of Peacock Room in home of F. R. Leyland (now in Freer Gallery). Exhibited several portraits, nocturnes at Grosvenor Gallery, including *The Falling Rocket*, which Ruskin attacked in *Fors Clavigera* ("flinging a pot of paint in the public's face"), thus frightening away buyers and sitters.

1878   Made first experiments in lithography; revived his interest in etching. Money troubles increased; pictures not sold were being pawned. Brought action against Ruskin for "pot of paint" attack; was awarded a farthing damages without costs.

1879   Expense of trial, and other losses brought about bankruptcy. Bailiffs took possession of the White House, his home in Chelsea. Left for Italy with commission from Fine Arts Society to produce twelve etchings of Venice. Before going, disposed of as many pictures as he could, left others with friends; many were never recovered.

1880 In Venice, worked mainly on etchings, pastels. Effects sold at Sotheby's. Returned to London. Exhibited Venice etchings at Fine Art Society; they were criticized as "unfinished."

1881 Exhibited Venice pastels. Met Oscar Wilde.

1882 Painted portraits, including Lady Archibald Campbell, Théodore Duret. Exhibited portrait at Salon. Met Sickert, who became pupil and assistant.

1883 Exhibited large group of etchings at Fine Art Society. *Mother* received third class medal at Salon. Painted small landscapes, seascapes at St. Ives.

1884 One man exhibition of oils, pastels, first large group of watercolors at Dowdeswell's Gallery. Visited Holland, spending some time at Dordrecht; made watercolors, etchings of Dutch subjects. Met Joseph Pennell, future biographer. Elected to Society of British Artists. Exhibited portraits at Salon.

1885 Delivered "Ten O'Clock" lecture in London, Cambridge, Oxford, etc. Exhibited two pictures at Salon. Painted small landscapes, seascapes at Dieppe (with Sickert).

1886 Dowdeswell's issued "Set of Twenty-Six Etchings," held second one-man exhibition of small oils, watercolors, pastels, drawings. Exhibited fifty small oils, watercolors, pastels in International Exhibition, Paris; other artists in exhibition included Monet, Pissarro, Sisley, Renoir, Morisot, Raffaelli, Rodin. Elected President, Society of British Artists.

1887 Secured Royal Charter for society, now Royal Society of British Artists. Renewed enthusiasm for lithography.

1888 In Paris, taken by Monet to meet Mallarmé to discuss translation of "Ten O'Clock." Compelled to resign from R.B.A. because of unpopular policies. Exhibited two paintings at Salon. Drifted apart from Maud. Married Beatrix Godwin, widow of his friend, E. W. Godwin, architect. Made watercolors, etchings in France. Elected Honorary Member, Royal Bavarian Academy.

1889 Sickert organized large restrospective exhibition of Whistler's work in College for Working Men and Women, London. Awarded first class medal at Munich, Cross of St. Michael of Bavaria; awarded gold medal at International Exhibition, Amsterdam; made Chevalier of Légion d'Honneur. Painted, etched in Holland.

1890 William Heinemann published collection of Whistler's earlier writings in *The Gentle Art of Making Enemies*. Mallarmé introduced Whistler to French critics Geffroy, Mirabeau, Delzant; formed committee to urge French government to buy *Mother* for nation.

1891 First sales to public collections: *Carlyle* portrait bought by Corporation of Glasgow; *Mother* bought for Luxembourg Museum, Paris.

1892 Retrospective exhibition at Goupil Gallery was complete success, more than regained recognition of British public, lost at time of Ruskin attack. Worked in Paris on etching, lithography.

1893 Settled in Paris. Began a number of portraits.

1894 Met Charles Freer of Detroit, later to become major Whistler collector.

1895 Returned to England for Mrs. Whistler's health. Produced small landscapes, seascapes, lithographs, etchings at Lyme Regis. Lithographs exhibited at Fine Art Society, well received. Honors at Venice international exhibition, gold medal at Antwerp.

1896 Mrs. Whistler died. Whistler went through period of great restlessness, traveling in Britain and on the continent, alternating residence in London and Paris from then on.

1898 Elected Chairman of executive council, then President, International Society of Sculptors, Painters and Gravers. Played key role in organizing first exhibition, including Rodin, Manet, Monet, Sisley, Toulouse-Lautrec, Bonnard, Vuillard. Greatly upset at death of Mallarmé. Opened short-lived art school in Paris. Worked on portraits and series of small nudes. Often ill.

1899 Special show of etchings included in second exhibition of International Society. Visited Italy, Holland.

1900 Paris International Exhibition, Grand Prix for painting and another for engraving. Painted in Ireland, Holland.

1901 Painted and etched in Mediterranean. Poor health. Continued working on small oils, watercolors, lithographs.

1902 Intermittently ill. Worked on portraits, mostly unfinished.

1903 Received honorary degree, Doctor of Laws, University of Glasgow. Died in London, July 17. Buried in Chiswick cemetery.

The literature on Whistler is vast and often inconsequential; mercifully, perhaps, most of it is out of print. An authoritative bibliography would be so enormous that it is beyond the scope of this book—and probably beyond the stamina of all but a few dedicated readers. Therefore, the purpose of this brief bibliographical note is simply to recommend a handful of books which I have found helpful and which seem a reasonable introduction to Whistler's life and work. Inevitably, the books overlap and often say the same things, but each has its own insights to contribute.

The best of Whistler's own writings (and the worst) will be found in *The Gentle Art of Making Enemies* (New York, 1967).

Four biographies are worth reading for a start. By far the best single book on the artist is James Laver's *Whistler* (London, 1930, revised 1951), authoritative, perceptive, and delightful to read. Hesketh Pearson's *The Man Whistler* (London, 1952) is a piece of elegant journalism, which reads like an extended magazine profile, and provides a swift survey of public fact and private rumor, sometimes debatable. *The World of James McNeill Whistler* by Horace Gregory (New York, 1959) is not meant to be an authoritative biography or historical study; but the author is a distinguished poet who was once an art student, and his insights have the special quality of one artist writing about another. The "basic" biography, written with the artist's cooperation, is the voluminous *The Life of James McNeill Whistler* by E. R. and J. Pennell (London and Philadelphia, 1908, last revision, Philadelphia, 1920); the book is required reading for the scholar, teems with facts, but is so worshipful that one must read it with more than a few grains of salt.

Denys Sutton has written two helpful volumes. *James McNeill Whistler: Paintings, Etchings, Pastels and Watercolours* (London, 1966) is an intelligent introduction to the artist's work and provides the best pictorial survey of his work in all media. *Nocturne: The Art of James McNeill Whistler* (London, New York, and Philadelphia, 1964) is particularly valuable for its examination of the artist's development, his influences, and his relation to the art of his time.

Two catalogs of recent Whistler exhibitions are extremely useful. Andrew McLaren Young's 1960 catalog, titled *James McNeill Whistler*, was compiled for an exhibition which he organized for The Arts Council of Great Britain and The English Speaking Union of the United States; the exhibition was shown at The Arts Council Gallery, London, and The Knoedler Gallery, New York. Frederick A. Sweet's *James McNeill Whistler* was compiled for a 1968 exhibition at The Art Institute of Chicago and the Munson-Williams-Proctor Institute, Utica, New York. The Young catalog contains an excellent annotated bibliography of virtually everything worth reading on the artist—up to 1960, the catalog's publication date. Both publications have good notes on pictures from major collections in America and the United Kingdom.

This highly personal bibliographical note would be incomplete without two other books, neither one about Whistler. My fascination with the period began when I ran across William Gaunt's *The Pre-Raphaelite Tragedy* (London, 1942), which presents a memorable picture of Whistler's world and the forces against which he was fighting. And to those who have read Rudolf Arnheim's *Art and Visual Perception* (Berkeley and Los Angeles, 1967), it should be obvious that this extraordinary book has influenced my interpretation of Whistler's achievement—and is essential reading for anyone who hopes to understand the revolutionary art of the late nineteenth and early twentieth centuries.

Nothing is more tempting than to gossip about James McNeill Whistler. Striding through the streets of Chelsea and Montmartre in patent leather pumps, decked out in colors that drove Degas to remark "If you were not a genius you would be the most ridiculous man in Paris," coiffed in calculated disarray with a single white lock trained to curl down his forehead, peering at pictures and people through a monocle like Groucho Marx glaring through his lensless glasses, swinging an outsize walking stick like a shillelagh (and sometimes using it for the same purpose), flattening his critics with verbal sidewinders that are still quoted a century later, Whistler was one of the great professional characters of the nineteenth century.

He loved publicity and he got lots of it. He worked hard to shock people; living in a more shockable age than our own, he succeeded in scandalizing as many people as a man could without the aid of television or mass magazines. He was a master of insult and his quarrels with Ruskin, Wilde, and a host of others became as famous as other men's duels and love affairs. With the possible exception of Degas, he was the wittiest man in the recorded history of art.

Yet the public and private Whistler were often at odds. He was a man of perpetual paradox.

He scoffed at religion, but never forgot that his New England mother wanted him to be a parson, diligently took her to church each Sunday, and kept his promise never to draw or paint on the Sabbath. A self-proclaimed genius in public, Whistler was obsessively self-critical in the studio, ruthlessly wiping out and repainting, grimly destroying piles of pictures which he might have sold, but which he considered failures. He dressed outlandishly, but designed stark interiors for his succession of homes—interiors that prefigured the international style in twentieth century architecture, much as his elegant, uncluttered book designs prefigured the typography of our own day. A bantam five-foot-four, he fascinated women, had a series of mistresses and a free-wheeling sex life before marrying in his fifties, but objected to nude models posing in co-ed classes of art students. He craved public recognition, but detested the art public, whom he badgered and baited into a hostility that matched his own—then brooded bitterly when his pictures failed to sell.

Born and educated in America, Whistler spent his entire mature life abroad, yet always regarded himself as an outsider to European society, which he found corrupt and ignorantly self-righteous. In fact, his best lines sound surprisingly like the most American wit of the day, Mark Twain. When a dissatisfied portrait sitter pointed to the canvas and asked Whistler if he considered *that* a great work of art, the painter shot back, "Do you consider yourself a great work of nature?" When the buyers of his great Carlyle portrait objected to the steep price for a figure that was not even life size, the painter observed, "Very few men are life size."

Whistler's wit and his flair for public display have led to frequent comparisons with his friend (and later his enemy) Oscar Wilde. But the analogy is superficial. A better comparison might be made with Ezra Pound, whose role in the history of English and American poetry is something like Whistler's role in the history of art. Both the poet and the painter were expatriates, unmistakably American, yet chose to live on alien soil. Both were not only artists of stature, but propagandists, crusaders against literary affectation, archaic romanticism, and Victorian pretension. Both advocated an art that was an intense response to life, personal, direct, modest in scale, and devoid of technical fireworks. Both delighted in encouraging the young and the unspoiled. And both were angry men, doomed to conflict and misunderstanding.

Whistler was a thoroughly ornery, thoroughly memorable man. A complete bibliography would be an Everest of legend and chitchat and "I remember when . . ." Quotable beyond a biographer's wildest dreams, he makes delightful copy. But this is precisely Whistler's problem: the artist is too easily upstaged by the man.

Having made the inevitable bow to Whistler the man, this slender book is an attempt to explain his achievement as a painter. For he shocked his contemporaries not merely by his public performances, but by his innovations on canvas. It was not in the Hogarth Club and the Café Royal, but in the silence of his studio that he groped for immortality.

In art as in politics, time is cruel to revolutionaries. The mad dogs of one era become the faithful sheep dogs of the next. The books tell us that the nineteenth century was an age of upheaval in painting, but we no longer feel the shock waves. More recent and more violent revolutionary movements—like cubism, expressionism, action painting, and a score of others—already seem remote; their products are already stacked away in the dusty pantheon of art history. In an age when upheaval is the norm, we find it hard to imagine why people were so shaken by Courbet, Manet, the impressionists, the Pre-Raphaelites. Courbet and Manet are upheld by today's academicians as the exemplars of good, solid, old fashioned painting. Impressionism is the style of millions of Sunday painters. And the sytle of the Pre-Raphaelites, once the scandal of London, now seems too innocuous even for children's books.

Among the experimental painters of the last century, few were more shocking to their contemporaries than Whistler, and none seems *less* shocking today.

The painters and sculptors of the French *avant-garde*—Courbet, Manet, Degas, Rodin—considered him their one comrade-in-arms in the hopelessly square English speaking world, the one major painter beyond the English Channel. (At Whistler's death, Rodin planned a monument which, like so many grandiose sculptural schemes, never came off.) The French literary *avant-garde* recognized Whistler as the visual artist whose goals came closest to their own. They idolized him. Mallarmé was the closest friend of Whistler's later years. Huysmans described his art as *"exquise, toute personnelle, toute neuve."* Proust wrote landscape descriptions in the manner of Whistler and treasured a lavender glove which the painter had left behind.

To the art public, Whistler's subdued and graceful paintings were every bit as shocking as the "brutal realism" of Courbet and Manet. Ruskin spoke for the Victorians when he called the American "a coxcomb . . . flinging a pot of paint in the public's face." To a generation which has seen the abstract expressionists *literally* flinging paint, the charge against Whistler seems laughable. On the contrary, his work now impresses us as the ultimate in restraint.

Yet the Victorians and their counterparts beyond the channel *were* outraged, and they knew why. Whistler's paintings represented the systematic negation of the values which his contemporaries had been trained to seek in art. His attitudes toward subject matter, toward pictorial design, toward color, toward paint itself—in fact, his concept of the purpose of painting—were the attitudes of the twentieth century, not of the nineteenth.

Despite his early allegiance to the "realism" of Courbet, his mentor, the lifelong thrust of Whistler's art was toward what we now call abstraction. In an era dominated by story telling pictures, Whistler declared war on subject matter and insisted that the painter's subject is painting. Like Turner and Monet, he gradually evolved an art in which the outlines of the visible world began to melt away and the language of painting began to emerge as an end in itself.

If the art public found Courbet, Manet, Degas, and the impressionists shocking, they found Whistler's mature work incomprehensible. An audience with a literary preoccupation could find *some* food for sexual fantasy in pictures of bathers, barmaids, ballet girls, and tarts scrubbing their backs. The impressionists did sometimes paint familiar Paris streets and beach resorts, however sloppy their style might seem. But Whistler's best work—the landscapes and seascapes of his final three decades—gave the viewer practically nothing to hold onto: no recognizable people, rarely a familiar landmark, no local color, no detail, no sense of perspective or three dimensional form. It was easy to see that Courbet, Manet, and Degas were dirty old men, that Monet and Pissarro were too lazy or incompetent to finish a painting; but Whistler was an outright fraud, trying to hoodwink the public with what Hazlitt (speaking of Turner) had condemned as "pictures of nothing."

Whistler expected his audience to respond simply to what they saw on the surface of the canvas: light and shade, color and texture, the subtle interplay of shapes on the picture plane. He was too early. Some did respond to the more explicit linear language of his etchings—which supported him while his paintings lay unsold in the studio—and to the portraits in which they could recognize someone they knew or wanted to know. In his fifties, when a lifetime of dusty pictures began to sell at last, there was a run on the portraits and figures; he was hailed as the greatest etcher of the day; but only a chosen few responded to the late landscapes and seascapes in which his abstract vision reached its ultimate development.

These are the paintings which today's non-figurative artists have rediscovered. The Whistler who now speaks most freshly to us is the visionary painter of the nocturnes which a baffled critic for the London *Times* said were "released from all functions of representations"; the aging Whistler who finally stripped his pictorial language to the bone and painted the small, stenographic, radically simplified sea pieces which were rarely appreciated in his own day and are rarely exhibited even now. Here Whistler is revealed as a key figure in the history of modern painting who (in Horace Gregory's words) "cleared the background for presenting non-objective art."

The nocturnes reproduced here will be familiar to some readers, less familiar to others. But the small coastal landscapes, the oil sketches and watercolors of Whistler's last two decades, may be a new and revealing experience. Like Constable's oil sketches, these tiny pictures have been largely ignored by the art public, but have enjoyed an underground reputation among painters, who have agreed with Sickert that "Whistler expressed the essence of his talent in his little panels—*pochades*, it is true, in measurement, but masterpieces of classic painting in importance."

A small, wiry, erect military figure stepped out of the crowd at the Royal Academy and paused before a canvas by Frith, the popular narrative painter. "Amazing!" cried a piercing, sardonic voice. "This picture tells a story! See, the little girl has a pussy cat, the other little girl has a dog—and that little girl has broken a toy; there are real tears rolling down her cheeks. Amazing!"

It was Whistler on the offensive. No one laughed. For he was not attacking a picture, but everyone in the room.

To the Victorians and to their contemporaries across the channel, painting was pictorial literature, a ponderous ballet of "types," not people. In judging a picture, the nineteenth century audience was trained to ask the kind of questions we might ask about a historical film. Are the faces and figures, costumes and settings appropriate to the event? Are the poses and gestures—the performances in this mummified drama—convincing? Would Socrates or Napoleon or Farmer Brown really look like that? What is the exact story behind this picture and, even more important, what is the moral?

No wonder people were horrified (and titillated) by Manet's *Dejeuner sur l'herbe.* Just what was that naked girl doing in a deserted park with those fully clothed men? Worse still, what was she *going* to do? A much more baffling canvas in the same exhibition was the most notorious picture of Whistler's youth, *The White Girl:* a picture of a girl in a white dress, standing before a white drapery, and holding a flower. What could the artist possibly *mean* by that ghostly effect of white on white? The British had thought the painting a crude attempt to illustrate Wilkie Collins' popular novel, *The Woman in White,* and Whistler had published a futile protest, denying any connection with any book. The French critic, Castagnary, after some head scratching over the supposed symbolism, came up with a more provocative interpretation: *The White Girl* was the bride contemplating her lost innocence on the morning after the wedding night. This time Whistler did not bother to protest; the public simply could not look at a picture without inventing a story.

But it was not Whistler's nature to remain silent for long. Unlike most artists, he was a propagandist by temperament. In the years that followed, he spoke out more boldly than any other painter for a view of art which history has tagged with the grotesque slogan, "art for art's sake."

"The vast majority of English folk cannot and will not consider a picture as a picture, apart from any story which it may be supposed to tell," he wrote in one of his many manifestos, "The Red Rag." "If they really could care for pictorial art at all, they would know that the picture should have its own merit, and not depend upon dramatic, or legendary, or local interest."

The analogy between music and painting, popularized by Pater, was widely discussed in *avant-garde* circles, but the public shrugged when Whistler declared: "As music is the poetry of sound, so is painting the poetry of sight, and the subject-matter has nothing to do with harmony of sound or colour."

These were not the words of a lily-clutching Victorian esthete, but the convictions of a tough minded New Englander, trained at West Point for a military career. Whistler was arguing for fundamentals. He was simply asking his readers to recognize that a painting is an object made out of paint. The essential question, therefore, was whether or not the object was well made, like the blue and white Chinese porcelains which Whistler collected.

"Art should be independent of all clap-trap," he insisted, "should stand alone, and appeal to the artistic sense of eye or ear, without confounding this with emotions entirely foreign to it, as devotion, pity, love, patriotism, and the like."

He saw a successful painting as the thrust, movement, countermovement, and final equilibrium of forms and colors in pictorial space—a fabric of paint, strong and tightly woven. "It seems to me," he wrote to Fantin-Latour in 1868, "that colour ought to be, as it were, embroidered on the canvas, that is to say, the same colour ought to appear in the picture continually here and there, in the same way that a thread appears in an embroidery, and so should all the others, more or less according to their importance. Look how well the Japanese understood this. They never look for contrast, on the contrary, they're after repetition."

Although Whistler had his doubts about the loosely designed pictures of Monet and Pissarro, the impressionists too wove a fabric of color out of rhythmic, repetitive "comma brush strokes." They wove rough wool, full of loops and slubs; Whistler wove silk.

If a painting was not a literary or moral force, but primarily a visual experience—a kind of man-made garden for the eye to stroll in—then the artist's relationship to nature was fundamentally changed. Nature was no longer a palace to which the artist must carry graven images in tribute, but a warehouse piled high with the raw materials of art, all there for the taking.

"Nature contains the elements, in colour and form, of all pictures, as the keyboard contains the notes of all music," Whistler said in the most famous of his public statements, the "Ten O'Clock" lecture delivered in 1888.

"But the artist is born to pick, and choose, and group with science, these elements, that the result may be beautiful—as the musician gathers his notes, and forms his chords, until he bring forth from chaos glorious harmony.

"To say to the painter, that Nature is to be taken as she is, is to say to the player, that he may sit on the piano.

"That Nature is always right, is an assertion, artistically, as untrue, as it is one whose truth is universally taken for granted. Nature is very rarely right, to such an extent even, that it might almost be said that Nature is usually wrong: that is to say, the condition of things that shall bring about the perfection of harmony worthy a picture is rare . . . seldom does Nature succeed in producing a picture."

This enormously influential statement—translated and spread abroad by Mallarmé, the most advanced artistic tastemaker on the continent—not only explained the philosophical basis of Cézanne (whom Whistler detested) but of all the art movements for whom Cézanne served as the fountainhead.

Nor was a painting intended to impress the viewer with the long, honest toil that went into its construction; with the huffing and puffing of the artist at work on the elaborate detail of the big salon pieces which were obviously worth thousands of guineas in sheer man-hours —in contrast to Whistler's pictures, which looked like no work at all.

"A picture is finished when all trace of the means used to bring about the end has disappeared.

"To say of a picture, as is often said in its praise, that it shows great and earnest labour, is to say that it is incomplete and unfit for view . . . for work alone will efface the footsteps of work.

"The work of the master reeks not of the sweat of the brow— suggests no effort—and is finished from its beginning.

"The masterpiece should appear as the flower to the painter— perfect in its bud as in its bloom—with no reason to explain its presence—no mission to fulfill—a joy to the artist—a delusion to the philanthropist—a puzzle to the botanist—an accident of sentiment and alliteration to the literary man."

This was more than an argument for the planned spontaneity of impressionism or expressionism or action painting. Whistler was proposing the unfamiliar idea that the artist was not paid for his labor but for his vision. Perhaps the most memorable moment in the painter's famous libel suit against Ruskin (over the "pot of paint" attack) came when the plaintiff was asked to justify a price tag of two hundred guineas for a picture which was "the labour of two days"; the drowsy audience was startled into spontaneous applause when he answered, "I ask it for the knowledge of a lifetime."

Whistler's flirtation with teaching was brief, but again he stressed the primacy of vision over craft. In an age which adored the virtuoso, he surprised the class by pointing to one girl's clumsy but vivid canvas: "She can't draw. She can't paint. But she doesn't need to."

It was too easy for Whistler's contemporaries (and for later critics) to brush aside his elegant prose as a plea for a cameo art, a precious parlor game of effete young men whom the painter despised.

"And now . . . the Dilettante stalks abroad. The amateur is loosed. The voice of the aesthete is heard in the land, and catastrophe is upon us.

"Shall this gaunt, ill-at-ease, distressed, abashed mixture of *mauvaise honte* and desperate assertion call itself artistic . . . while the artist, in fullness of heart and head, is glad, and laughs aloud, and is happy in his strength, and is merry at the pompous pretension—the solemn silliness that surrounds him."

When Wilde, with whom Whistler is too often compared, showed the painter a poem written on a gossamer tissue, the American commented in disgust, "It's worth its weight in gold."

Far from advocating a gutless, hermetic art, removed from life, Whistler demanded that the artist discover "the beautiful in all conditions and in all times, as did . . . Rembrandt, when he saw picturesque grandeur and noble dignity in the Jews' quarter of Amsterdam, and lamented not that its inhabitants were not Greeks."

Whistler's crusade was not against story telling, but against corn. He believed in paintings of real, robust people like "Tintoret and Paul Veronese"; he worshiped Velazquez; and he always insisted that the social commentaries of Hogarth were the greatest art produced in England. He loved the Dutch "little masters," who painted relaxed, intimate views of real people, not types, in real surroundings.

The American's strongest early influence was, after all, Courbet, who naturally exaggerated the case for painting the real world: "Ugliness is beauty!" Whistler's first pictures of the Thames, his lifelong obsession, were created (as Hesketh Pearson says) "in the midst of barges, sailors, dockers, land rats, and water rats . . . he was discovering beauty where his contemporaries could see only ugliness, and creating romance out of industry." His late art, at its most abstract, was the product of a memory systematically trained to record and edit the details of the visible world.

Whistler described the young Sargent—a brilliant landscape painter forced to earn his living as a virtuoso portrait painter—as "an acrobat in pain." But Whistler might have said the same of his own struggles with the human form.

He won early attention in the 1860s for pictures of striking girls ("stunners" in Victorian slang) playing the piano, looking at Chinese porcelain, studying the mirror, just standing or sitting in an oriental robe. For the rest of his life, he strove painfully to build on this early success with the figure.

"Whistler began hundreds of portraits," says James Laver. "He finished about a dozen." A handful of his portraits are masterpieces, but Whistler recognized that the human figure was not his strong point. He tried portraiture again and again throughout his life; reduced his sitters to tears of rage, hunger, and fatigue as they were forced to submit to dozens of unsuccessful sittings; choked back his own tears of frustration as he drew and redrew Mrs. Frederick Leyland's hands and failed to get her husband's legs right; scraped out, scrubbed out, slashed canvases, and ultimately gave up large scale portraits almost entirely, generally restricting himself to small, casual studies in his final years.

There were two reasons for Whistler's tortured career as a portraitist.

He frankly admitted his lack of academic figure drawing skill. The American sculptor, Frederick MacMonnies, suggested, with understandable trepidation, that Whistler had drawn a leg too short, and was astonished by the painter's gratitude. "What an eye for a line a sculptor has," said Whistler in admiration.

But there was a more profound reason: the human form simply did not cooperate in Whistler's search for a radically new kind of vision. Likeness, characterization, accurate drawing, a revealing and unconventional pose, a powerful abstract design, spontaneity of technique, a uniquely personal kind of paint quality—he wanted them all and it was just asking too much. Only Velazquez had come close and Whistler felt hopelessly inferior to the Spanish master he adored. When a gushing lady admirer compared the American to the great Spaniard, Whistler growled, "Why bring in Velazquez?" Only his friends knew that this was not arrogance, but self-contempt.

When they were first shown, Whistler's portraits did win great notoriety (but few sales) for their bare designs, lack of detail, close tonalities, and evanescent paint quality. The pictures eventually came to occupy prominent places in leading museums on both sides of the Atlantic. But the public has lost interest in most of the portraits. Besides, the ravages of time have made it harder and harder to enjoy many of these paintings. Particularly in his mature portraits of the 1870s, the grisly paint chemistry of the last century has conspired with Whistler's own lack of interest in the chemical behavior of paint. (Asphalt was used to paint pictures, not to build roads, and manufacturers literally ground up mummies and collected camel urine to make artists' colors.) Tragically, in many of his best portraits, subtlety has given way to invisibility and the best conservators have found no way to revive color which is just not there to be revived.

However, despite their decay, the portraits of the 1870s tell us a great deal about Whistler's working methods and goals. Furthermore, his sitters were often articulate people and have left us first hand accounts of the creative torment they witnessed. Although the portraits are not really the focus of this book, these accounts are important because they are our most reliable record of how Whistler worked—simply because someone (the sitter) is there when a portrait is painted, while the artist is more often alone when he paints a landscape or seascape.

Whistler planned a portrait like a cavalry charge against heavy odds, an assault against an enemy entrenched on high ground. Although he rarely made preliminary drawings to be "squared up" and enlarged onto the canvas, he had the portrait completely visualized in the mind's eye before he touched a brush. The pose was adjusted with great care; the few accessories were painstakingly selected and placed. The studio was bare of all visual distraction. The color scheme was likely to hinge upon the closest tonal relationships of neutrals—grays, tans, browns, blacks—and was decided in advance. The canvas was toned with a veil of color that would envelop and harmonize the colors that followed. Each hue was pre-mixed before the painting began, rather than mixed on the palette as the job progressed. Minor adjustments would be made by wiping, scraping, and mixing on the canvas itself. Knowing that everything depended on a bold, decisive attack—and that his chances of victory were slim—Whistler left as little as possible to chance.

Then the charge was sounded. The artist quickly made two chalk marks on the canvas—for the highest and lowest points of the figure—stepped far back, seized a large brush, two or three feet long, and attacked the surface with big, sweeping strokes. He held the gargantuan brush at arm's length, standing far back to see the picture as a total design. After a few moments, he stepped back across the room to scan the field of battle, regrouped his forces and charged again. The complete distribution of pictorial elements was accomplished in a series of rushes, within an hour or two. Then the rushes would become briefer, the brushes smaller, the strokes less fierce, less broad. The completion of the portrait then became a matter of slight touches here and there, with long pauses for study in between. Robert de Montesquiou-Fezensac reported that the artist would slowly bring a brush close to the canvas, change his mind, drop the brush, and reach for another, seeking precisely the right tool for the final accents on which the painter risks everything. Montesquiou said that the canvas was touched no more than fifty times in a three hour sitting, "each stroke lifting a veil from the sketch."

Then, when the last touch had been placed and the portrait seemed perfect, the sitter, drooping after endless hours of posing, would watch in horror as the artist reached for a rag and scrubbed the whole thing out! The battle was not finished after all. That madman, Whistler, had seen some imperfection, invisible to anyone but him, and insisted on starting all over again. Many sitters walked out in disgust

and never returned. Just as often, the artist gave up in disgust, after trying again and again. No one knows how many portraits he abandoned midway or destroyed. Lady Archibald Campbell, who sat for a long series of studies, said: "The first impression thrown on the canvas he often put away, often destroyed." Years later, when she asked the artist about one of her favorites, "he laughed, and said he had destroyed her."

This weird performance, the TV version of an eccentric artist, was the closest thing to action painting in the nineteenth century. It was an attempt to see a large picture as a totality, a dynamic whole from the very beginning; to place a complete vision on the canvas instantaneously and to retain the initial freshness, ruggedness, and power of this vision to the very end. Like the great sumi-e painters of Japan or the abstract expressionists of our own day, his strategy was to get it right the first time or repaint it. One mis-step and he started from scratch.

Theodore Duret, one of Whistler's most perceptive sitters, watched ten tries before his portrait was completed. He was among the few to understand how hard Whistler worked to make his pictures look effortless: "One of his principle anxieties . . . was to preserve . . . the appearance of having been produced without effort . . . Therefore that with which his detractors have reproached him, the painting of sketches only, was not with him the consequence of absence of effort, but came from his very conception of a work of art, and was on the contrary the result of persistent attention and additional labor."

Whistler's goals in portrait painting—about which he was most articulate, perhaps because portraiture was a recurring nightmare—are significant primarily because they were the goals that he finally reached in his more consistently successful landscapes and seascapes.

From the very beginning, he was hesitant to call them portraits. The word, abstraction, was not available to him, but he knew that his mature portraits were pictures in which the human figure served as a motif in an abstract drama. When the French critic, Paul Mantz, called *The White Girl* a symphony, Whistler seized on the word and used it in several titles. He also called some of his pictures harmonies. The night pieces were first called moonlights, but he finally preferred nocturnes, a word suggested by Frederick Leyland, to whom the artist wrote: "I say I can't thank you too much for the name 'Nocturne' as a title for my moonlights. You have no idea what an irritation it proves to the critics and consequent pleasure to me—besides it is really charming and does so poetically say all I want to say and *no more* than I wish."

The closest he came to a non-musical word was *arrangement*. He called the famous portrait of his mother an *Arrangement in Grey and Black*: "To me it is interesting as a picture of my mother; but what can or ought the public to care about the identity of the portrait? It must stand or fall on its merits as an 'arrangement,' and it very nearly fell; that's a fact."

The essence of a successful arrangement was a dynamic, yet balanced relationship between the silhouette of the figure and its background, between positive and negative shapes, as the twentieth century artist calls them.

This, in turn, demanded not only careful design of the pose as a flat shape, but the flattening of the figure itself by the elimination of traditional lighting, the so-called *chiaroscuro* of the old masters. The "normal" method of lighting was to place a light source somewhat to the side and slightly above the subject, so that some planes were in light and others were in shadow; the effect was to throw the forms into relief, to emphasize three dimensionality, like a photograph of a piece of sculpture. But Whistler placed the sitter in a frontal or diffused light, thereby minimizing the play of light and shade that made the figure look round. In this sort of light, the figure was reduced to flat patches of tone and color.

But this flattening of form presents a new difficulty. As Denys Sutton points out, "One problem which challenges the portrait painter is the presentation of the whole figure so that it naturally inhabits the space allotted to it and does not take on the appearance of a playing card—as do many seventeenth-century journeyman portraits."

To avoid this paper cutout look, the experienced painter knows that he must pay careful attention to what he calls edges—where one shape ends and another begins. Painters speak of soft and hard, lost and found edges: Whistler had studied Rembrandt and Velazquez, in whose mature work the transition from figure to background was almost always soft or lost. That is, the painter had consciously blurred these transitions, thrown them out of focus, blended background color into the edge of a face or a sleeve so that there was no precise line where one ended and the other began.

Rembrandt, in particular, had carried the process one step further by darkening the background, making it so close in value to the figure that it became increasingly difficult to distinguish the figure from its surroundings. And both the Dutch and Spanish masters had chosen backgrounds that were devoid of detail, neutral in color, and spatially ambiguous. The viewer could not say that it was a sky or a wall or a drapery, placed somewhere in space: it was just a shadowy color that surrounded the figure like murky air.

Whistler adapted these methods to his own special needs by painting the sitter as he might look in the failing light of a late afternoon in winter. The edges of the silhouette were blurred; colors became muted; light tones were darkened and dark tones lightened by this strange, gray-brown, unifying light.

This dying light subdued or eliminated all distracting detail that might interfere with his bold design of large, flat shapes. "As the light fades and the shadows deepen all petty and exacting details vanish, everything trivial disappears, and I see things as they are in great strong masses: the buttons are lost, but the sitter remains; the garment is lost, but the sitter remains; the sitter is lost, but the shadow remains; the shadow is lost, but the picture remains. And that, night cannot efface from the painter's imagination."

What emerged was the eerie continuity of color which he had recommended to Fantin-Latour, the feeling that everything in the picture was made of tinted smoke. "In a mature work of art," says Rudolf Arnheim, "all things seem to resemble each other. Sky, sea, ground, trees, and human figures begin to look as though they were made of one and the same substance, which falsifies the nature of nothing but recreates everything by subjecting it to the unifying power of the great artist."

Such paintings demanded a new kind of relationship between the audience and the work of art. The virtuoso portrait painters of the day bombarded the gallery-goer with big, bright salon pieces which clamored for attention: the portrait subject virtually stepped out of the frame and forced himself on the viewer's company. But Whistler insisted that the subject "should really, and in truth absolutely does, stand *within* the frame—and at a depth behind it equal to the distance at which the painter sees his model."

What Whistler was really suggesting was that the audience play a more active and perceptive role in the creative process. If the painting will not reach out and collar him, then the viewer must step forward —into the picture, if you will—and immerse himself in its atmosphere. Like the Japanese participating in the tea ceremony, the viewer must be prepared to examine and appreciate great subtleties which are not apparent to the casual onlooker, but which reveal themselves only after prolonged and dedicated contemplation.

Whistler was asking for a new kind of art public: an audience trained to respond to the language of painting and prepared to do some work. Once again, he was asking too much. His contemporaries had been raised on brass bands, not chamber music.

In the nocturnes of the late 1860s and the 1870s, the half light of the studio gave way to night, and Whistler painted the most controversial pictures of his career.

The nineteenth century viewer (like ourselves) was the inheritor of a fantastically complex system of picture making, rooted in the Renaissance, refined and elaborated over half a millennium. Although he took them all quite for granted, he had been trained unconsciously in the most complicated set of visual conventions in the history of art.

For the nineteenth century audience, the picture frame was a window looking out into a world of deep space, reaching to the horizon. The vista from the window *could* be hopelessly confusing: things in front of things, things behind things, people and objects (big and little) cutting in front of one another and half concealed, all with spaces in between, spaces that might be an inch or a mile or seven leagues. To most civilizations, such a picture would be pure chaos; they would prefer to bring everything up front, close to the window, lined up side by side so the viewer could really see what they look like. But the jumble beyond the picture window did make sense to the nineteenth century audience (as it does to us) because they had been educated to read an elaborate series of visual cues that worked for *them*, even though such cues might not work for people in other cultures.

For example, the viewer had learned a minor branch of geometry, called linear perspective, which permitted him to follow the lines in the picture, as he would a code, and thus figure out where things were: near, far, or somewhere in between. Having learned to read this imaginary grid of receding lines, he was not surprised by foreshortening; that is, he was not confused when an arm pointed straight at him, so that the fingers looked like a jumble of sausages—he still saw it as an arm. He also knew that the painter would help him locate forms in space by lining them up in planes, one behind the other, like rows of soldiers advancing, organizing themselves into foreground, middle ground, and background. And he had learned a color system, called atmospheric perspective, whereby the artist represents near objects as warmer, darker, or more intense than distant objects—which grow cooler, paler, and less intense in color as they approach the horizon. He also expected a painter to render nearby objects in sharply focused detail, while distant objects might lack detail and definition.

But the nocturnes virtually abandon all this. Whistler asked this audience to look at a canvas which was hardly more than a bluish, grayish, brownish, or blackish mist. Across this mist might jut a few blurry forms, dividing the space into what might be water and sky, or near and far, but it was hard to tell. Or the darkness might congeal here and there into a form that might be a building, a bridge, a ship, or a shoreline; but there were barely any details or sharp edges to identify the subject exactly. Sometimes there was a bit of atmospheric perspective—dark things that seemed to be in front of pale things—but no really definable space in between. Often there were just dark areas and light areas which might blur into one another so that one was not even sure where objects ended and space began. In fact, most of the picture might be mere space, just a blue-gray blank.

Whistler's contemporaries thought the nocturnes must be some perverse joke, like the holes in Henry Moore's sculpture or the cockeyed features in Picasso's faces. People were not being facetious when they asked "What is it?" or hung a nocturne upside down.

Here was one of those conflicts of perception which are often turning points in the history of the arts.

Whistler was proposing a new definition of space. He was suggesting that the viewer suspend his habitual definition of space as a sort of glass block with objects embedded in it; a three dimensional block whose face was locked into the picture frame and whose far side butted up against the distant horizon. Instead, Whistler asked that the viewer imagine space as the two dimensional surface of the painting; on this surface, shapes and colors might be arranged to suggest a third dimension lying beyond the picture frame, but the artist's primary job was to organize flat shapes on this flat surface (or picture

plane) to produce a satisfying design.

To maintain the integrity of the picture plane, the major elements in the painting are arranged parallel to the four edges of the canvas in a way which seems to "anticipate the two-dimensional abstraction of Mondrian," as Andrew McLaren Young points out. Shorelines, bridges, ships, and buildings line up as horizontals and verticals, with slight deviations to the diagonal for variety. A boat or a wall rarely plunges into deep space, toward the horizon, unless the painter carefully flattens its shape and reduces it to a near silhouette which lies quietly on the picture plane.

Whistler's detractors said that his pictures had no composition. But to the nineteenth century gallery-goer, composition was likely to mean the organization of pictorial elements to enhance the drama of a story, like the arrangement of actors on a stage. In contrast to this notion, Whistler proposed that composition—perhaps design is a better word—become an end in itself.

At one moment, he might try to move the viewer by the pure drama of positive shapes (land masses, walls, hulls and masts) interacting with negative space (sea and sky). Or like the oriental masters he admired, he might ask his audience to respond to a design decision so bold, yet so simple, that it seemed like no decision at all—the decision to leave much of the picture a series of large, unbroken areas of flat color, like the blank panels of a kakemono, or the expanse of bare paper, slashed with a few well placed strokes, in a sumi-e painting. He had discovered the power of negative space, the parts of the picture where things were *not*.

At still other times, he hoped to enchant the viewer with the ambiguities of space, when darkness or diffused light all but destroyed the distinction between positive and negative and the eye played a game of "now you see it, now you don't." (He had hinted at this game at the beginning of his career, when he painted what Courbet called "an apparition" of a white clad girl standing before an equally white curtain.)

But it was a game that few were willing to play. Tom Taylor, former London *Times* critic and editor of *Punch*, testified at the Ruskin trial that the nocturnes were "one step nearer to pictures than graduated tints on a wall-paper," and let it go at that.

Whistler's method of painting the nocturnes was as unconventional as the paintings themselves.

T. R. Way, who printed many of Whistler's lithographs, describes a walk with the artist, who stopped suddenly and "pointing to a group of buildings in the distance, an old public house at the corner of the road, with windows and shops showing golden lights through the gathering mist of the twilight, said, 'Look!' As he did not seem to have anything to sketch or make notes on, I offered him my notebook. 'No, no, be quiet,' was the answer; and after a long pause he turned and walked back a few yards; then, with his back to the scene at which I was looking, he said, 'Now see if I have learned it,' and repeated a full description of the scene, even as one might repeat a poem one had learned by heart."

Whistler was methodically training his memory according to the principles of a great and forgotten teacher, Lecoq de Boisbaudran. Whistler had not studied with him, but Legros and Fantin-Latour had. These two closest friends of the American's formative years in Paris must have described Lecoq's unique teaching method. "Lecoq conducted his last series of classes in the open air," says Horace Gregory, "in woods along the Seine, while models strolled through the sunlight and shade. While the models rested, students were required to reconstruct from memory what they had lately seen, the walking figures, the glancing of light between the leaves."

Lecoq had taught "that the imagination does no more than fuse the material furnished to it by the memory, thus producing completely new compounds." Equally important, Whistler had discovered that painting from memory—with the occasional aid of a few scribbled compositional notes—radically simplified the image that emerged on the canvas. Details dropped away. The mind retained only the big, bold shapes, the abstract structure of the subject, suppressing trivia and reducing the pictorial design to a pattern of essentials. If this abstract structure was right, neither detail nor finish mattered much. The job was to put the right shape in the right place, and Whistler was one of the first artists to acknowledge the role of the unconscious in making such decisions. Whether he knew it or not, he was also following the classic method of the Chinese landscape painters when he said, "Painting from nature should be done in the studio."

Back in the studio, the attack on the canvas followed the same strategy as that of the portraits. The colors were mixed in advance: for one seascape, he is said to have spent three days mixing his paints and perhaps an hour painting the picture. The paints were heavily diluted, almost to the consistency of Chinese ink, and were "different tones in the dominant colour of the picture," according to Denys Sutton. (This extreme dilution with turpentine or petrol may have been good picture making, but it was bad chemistry, and accounts for the poor preservation of many of Whistler's canvases.) The "sauce," as the painter called it, was so thin and runny that it might actually drip down the face of the canvas as he worked; sometimes he liked the effect and left the "accident" unchanged.

The only canvas that could hold such paint—without the "sauce" running off like water on a sheet of glass—was highly absorbent. The fluid color settled into the fibers of the canvas (previously toned to establish the underlying color of the design) like ink soaking into the blotter-like paper of the sumi-e painters. The effect of the absorbent canvas was to hold Whistler's fluid stroke intact, yet soften it and integrate it with the total fabric of color. This combination of fluidity and absorbency was the key to Whistler's unique paint quality: the feeling that the image was a veil of color, composed of decisive but unobtrusive strokes that never interrupted the intricate weave.

Although the attack was similar to that of action painting, the final effect was, of course, far from the raw power of abstract expressionism. Whistler, too, favored the big gestural stroke, the touch of the brush that had the premeditated spontaneity of calligraphy, but he took great pains "to save disturbing and embarrassing the canvas." In action painting, the excitement may be the visible evidence of the battle that has taken place on the canvas. Whistler, on the contrary, labored to eradicate every trace of the struggle. A shape may have been painted with a few massive sweeps of the brush, but as the Pennells point out, "How many times he made and wiped out that sweeping tone is another matter." All that remains in the wash of color is the faint imprint of the bristles, suggesting a casualness that denies the methodical planning and the ferocity of the attack. What emerges is a paradox: an art of nuance and suggestion, created at white heat.

Whistler's reputation as a painter is based mainly on the portraits and nocturnes produced in the 1860s and 1870s. The last two decades of the century were the final years of his career, when his fame was growing rapidly and money was less of a problem. In these years, he painted few large pictures—few survive, at least—but concentrated on small landscapes and seascapes, did an occasional small portrait, and produced lithographs which look surprisingly like Vuillard.

Most critics have suggested that he spent those years resting on his laurels, that he had run out of steam. In reality, the small pictures of this period were not only a distillation of Whistler's achievement—a summing up of all that he had learned—but embodied experiments that went beyond the nocturnes in their freshness and daring.

Eric Hoffer has said that man's greatest intellectual leaps are made in the mood of play. In such a mood, Whistler wrote to Paul Deschamps that he was "doing a lot of curious little 'games.'" Whistler's late paintings are genuinely playful, dashed off with casual certainty, as the nocturnes were not. Like Constable, whose little oil sketches are far more direct and exciting than his big easel paintings, Whistler felt really free to experiment on a small scale. On a panel no bigger than a sheet of note paper, the smallest touch of the brush looms large and registers the slightest impulse of the mind without labor. A swing of the wrist and a mile of shoreline is painted. The artist can gamble outrageously, for the stakes are low and a flick of the rag wipes away failure.

The differences between the small studies of the 1880s and 1890s and the earlier nocturnes are significant. The late pictures were not an aging artist's final holiday, but a voyage of discovery. The nocturnes (as well as the portraits) tend toward the monochromatic: painted in variations of a single color or in a closely related family of colors, they suggest more color than is really there. The distinction between positive shapes and negative space—when there is a distinction—is more often a contrast of light against dark than a contrast of colors. For this reason, at least some of the nocturnes reproduce reasonably well in a black and white photograph; the subtleties may be lost, but the large pattern is there.

In the most interesting of the late pictures, the interplay of dark and light gives way to color: not just warm and cool grays, browns and blacks, but blues, greens, pinks, ochres. In many of them, tonal contrast is abandoned entirely for color relationships which are so close in value that they barely register in a black and white photograph. There is no longer a pattern of positive and negative elements: space becomes pure color.

The picture is often divided into a series of horizontal strips of color, sometimes no more than three that represent sand, sea, and sky. The strips tend to fuse where they meet, forming a continuous fabric of paint, with minute variations in color suggesting the spatial shift from one section of terrain to the next. A few touches of color may suggest figures or ships just to steer the eye or to indicate scale.

Like Turner—who had also experimented with three blurred horizontal strips of color in his late watercolors—Whistler had chosen the water's edge for his most innovative pictures. Here space becomes a subject in itself, continuous, ambiguous, dissolving objects in a diffused light that abolishes edges, defies interruption, and insists on becoming a field of modulated color, a field of paint.

In these small paintings, Whistler came as close to total abstraction as any artist of his day. Yet, oddly enough, they were painted on the spot. After a lifetime of methodically constructing and reconstructing pictorial designs in the studio, Whistler at last felt free to sit on the beach and paint in the open air. The very power of these "thumb box paintings"—so far from Whistler's early attempts to match the "realism" of Courbet—stems from this direct contact with the subject. Unlike the calculated product of the studio, these final pictures are the product of real, not planned, spontaneity. They are the aging artist's relaxed, immediate response to the real world: abstractions painted from nature.

Sickert, writing with a painter's insight, caught the essence of Whistler's achievement: "The relation and keeping of the tone is marvellous in its severe restriction. It is this that is strong painting. No sign of effort, with immense result. He will give you in a space nine inches by four an angry sea, piled up, and running in, as no painter ever did before. The extraordinary beauty and truth of the relative colours, and the exquisite precision of the spaces, have compelled infinity and movement into an architectural formula of eternal beauty. Never was instrument better understood and more fully exploited than Whistler has understood and exploited oil paint in these panels. He has solved in them a problem that has hitherto seemed insoluble: to give a result of deliberateness to a work done in a few hours from Nature. It was the admirable preliminary order in his mind, the perfect peace at which his art was with itself, that enabled him to aim at and bring down quarry which, to anyone else, would have seemed intangible, and altogether elusive."

"You have done too much of the exquisite not to have earned more despair than anything else," wrote Henry James to Whistler.

The public saw the American painter as a carefree privateer, always ready for a scrap, delighted to take on the biggest man-o-war afloat; few saw Whistler in the studio, where the act of creation was too often a struggle against despair.

William Rothenstein describes an evening with Whistler in the late 1890s. "Climbing the stairs we found the studio in darkness. Whistler lighted a single candle. He had been gay enough during dinner, but now he became very quiet and intent, as though he forgot me. Turning a canvas that faced the wall, he examined it carefully, up and down, with the candle held near it, and then did the like with some others, peering closely into each. There was something tragic, almost frightening, as I stood and waited, in watching Whistler; he looked suddenly old, as he held the candle with trembling hands, and stared at his work, while our shapes threw restless, fantastic shadows, all around us. As I followed him silently down the stairs I realised that even Whistler must often have felt his heart heavy with the sense of failure."

He was obsessed with the need to destroy his failures and hated the sight of many of his pictures. He described one portrait as "damnable," something that might have "been done by my worst and most incompetent enemy . . . There must be no record of this abomination!" Toward the end of his life, he had the entire contents of his Paris studio shipped to him in London, where he methodically burned stacks of drawings and paintings.

Sometimes he could not face the pain of such destruction. Sickert recounts a poignant moment on the way to dinner at the end of a day's painting. As they walked down the street, Whistler suddenly halted: "You go back," he said to the young painter. "I shall only be nervous and begin to doubt again. Go back and take it all out." While the old man waited below, Sickert climbed the stairs and carefully wiped away the picture with a rag and benzoline.

"All along have I carefully destroyed plates, torn up proofs, and burned canvases," Whistler said quite frankly, ". . . that the future collector shall be spared the mortification of cataloguing his pet mistakes." He saw this destruction as a bid for immortality: "To destroy is to remain."

His very work method—painting and repainting until he got it right or gave it up—was an agony of self-doubt. "It's always the same—work that's so hard and uncertain," he wrote to Fantin-Latour. "I am so *slow*. When will I achieve a more rapid way of painting . . . I produce so little, because I rub out so much."

Working at white heat, ill-trained in drawing, relying on intuition but never sure that intuition was enough, he fantasized: "Ah! if only I had been a pupil of Ingres." The most intuitive of painters longed for the guidance of the most systematic.

Ingres was the last of the great painters for whom painting was a system, an orderly procedure like building a sculpture on an armature; he was, indeed, the last of the great sculptural painters, for whom drawing an arm was a problem in rendering the third dimension, as an architect renders a marble column. For Whistler (as for Degas), Ingres symbolized painting as a reliable body of professional knowledge, practical, tempting, but alas, no longer valid. Cézanne had said that it took him twenty years to learn that painting was not sculpture: this was precisely the problem of Whistler and the other experimental painters of his day. To give up sculptural painting was to give up the security of a system, to abandon the comforts of home port and set sail for uncharted waters.

Perhaps the simplest way to define an experimental artist is to say just this: his destination is out of sight and the available charts will not get him there. All he can do is set sail and expect to get lost again and again before he gets where he is going—if he ever gets there at all. He has no precedent to rely on, has met no one who has been there before him. Somewhere he may run across fragmentary reports of forgotten travelers who passed nearby (as Whistler found in the art of Japan and China); these tantalizing hints may be important clues or may lead him astray. Only when he sees land heave up on the horizon does he know he has arrived. Even then, he may not be able to repeat the trip without getting lost once again.

Degas, too, used the analogy of the journey when he said: "In our beginnings Fantin, Whistler and I were on the same road, the road from Holland. Go and see . . . a small picture, a *scène de toilette* by Fantin: we could have signed it, Whistler and I." They both quit the road and took to the steep rocks, struggling to clear paths of their own. Their tactics were surprisingly similar. Whistler literally wore his canvases out, painting and scrubbing away the same image a dozen times. Degas drew and redrew the same image, tossing aside sheet after sheet, each with a subtle variation of the theme.

By definition, the experimenter is a man doomed to fail more often than he succeeds. (When he begins to succeed more often than he fails, he is no longer an experimenter: he has evolved a system.) The experimenter's agony is that the day's work is chancy, his output uneven, his accomplishment hard to assess. How do we evaluate a life's work that is all peaks and valleys, not the usual lumpy plateau? Do we average out the peaks and valleys and see how high a plateau we get? What is there to say of the artist who dares more often than he succeeds? Which looms larger in history, the dare or the success? Is it just possible that *some* valleys are more important than the peaks?

Purely on the basis of his pictures, Whistler is not one of the supreme painters of his century. Turner and Degas and Cézanne also deserted the road and took to the rocks, but they climbed higher peaks. The gods of art history are outnumbered by those who did a small thing well—Vermeer, de Hoogh, Guardi, Corot, Vuillard, make your own list—and Whistler is one of these. Even this is a rare achievement.

But the second string masters of art history are rarely revolutionaries; they are more likely to work at perfecting existing styles.

More vocal than Turner or Cézanne, more willing to take the punishment of public life than Degas, Whistler *was* a revolutionary: he set out to change his world with pictures and with words. Most artists just go their own way, do their work, and hope that someone will buy it; they have neither the talent nor the temperament for public debate. Whistler, however, leaped into the spotlight which greater artists shunned. He not only painted in a new way, but he took on the job of defending, explaining, and promoting the advanced art of his time. He fought on all fronts: on the printed page, on the speaker's platform, in the courtroom, as well as on canvas.

He attacked the dominant esthetic assumptions of the day. Ruskin, the most influential spokesman for the establishment, had said that the function of true art was "praise," that the artist's duty was "truth to nature"; Whistler insisted that the artist's only responsibility was to be true to his vision. The academy was committed to anecdotal painting; Whistler lacked the firepower to lay siege to the establishment, but was a master of guerrilla warfare.

He asked painters and their public to consider esthetic questions which were to become major issues for artists and viewers in our own time. How much can the artist expect of his audience? How radically can the artist redesign, simplify, and transform the visible world? What is form? What is space? What are color and value and how do they interact to create form and space? What is paint itself? How important is the gesture of the brush, the painter's "handwriting?"

Whistler's own pictures put these questions in graphic form and served to focus the debate. Thus, the paintings, the failures as well as the successes, take on an importance beyond themselves. His achievement looms larger than his pictures.

Despite his role as a kind of midwife at the birth of abstract painting, Whistler is one of the great loners of art history. He remains an ambiguous figure because he does not fit any of the usual words for the nineteenth century *avant-garde;* his peers respected him from afar as painter and spokesman, but his experiments seemed to have very little connection with theirs. For a brief moment, he looked like a realist, an impressionist, an American Manet with a Pre-Raphaelite tinge, but not for long. He is not a post-impressionist, a symbolist, an *intimiste;* all the words contain a germ of truth, but go wide of the mark. He defies classification. For years, his work has existed in a no-man's-land between the Victorian era and our own. Now, to a generation which has seen non-figurative painting and felt the full impact of the questions raised by Whistler's work, this no-man's-land may be accessible at last.

"The master stands in no relation to the moment at which he occurs," said Whistler, "a monument of isolation—hinting at sadness —having no part in the progress of his fellow men." But the goddess, art, "is proud of her comrade, and promises that in after-years, others shall pass that way, and understand."

Color Plates

Plate 1

THE COAST OF BRITTANY

Oil on canvas

34⅜"x46" (87.2x116.7 cm.)

Signed and dated 1861

Wadsworth Atheneum, Hartford, Connecticut

Deeply impressed by the work of Courbet and his circle, Whistler began as a "realist." *The Coast of Brittany*—first exhibited at the Royal Academy in 1862 with the anecdotal title, *Alone with the Tide*—seems, at first glance, to be in the Courbet tradition. The rocks give the illusion of solidity and weight; they appear to be divided into planes of light and shadow, carefully modeled to accentuate their blockiness. Even the inward curve of the wave is carefully graded from dark to light to emphasize its three dimensionality.

But, at second glance, the picture looks less and less like the work of a follower of Courbet and begins to reveal the qualities that were to emerge in Whistler's mature paintings.

The rocks are far flatter than they seem. Few of them are actually modeled in planes of light and shade; nearly all of them are actually patches of broken color, edged here and there with a dark line to strengthen the forms and hint at shadows that are hardly there at all.

Typical, too, of the later Whistler are the high horizon line and the placement of the dominant forms in the upper half of the canvas. Even more striking is the contrast between the dark forms of the rocks and the blank, staring sand in the foreground; the entire lower third of the picture is vacant of any form except for the girl reclining on the rocks, plus an occasional stray boulder.

Even in this earliest of his major marine subjects, Whistler revealed his growing interest in the discrete placement of color, and in pictorial designs based on the interplay of form and large areas of negative space.

Plate 2

THE BLUE WAVE: BIARRITZ

Oil on canvas
24½"x34½" (62.2x87.6 cm.)
Signed and dated 1862
Hill-Stead Museum, Farmington, Connecticut

Whistler's second major seascape again reveals the debt to Courbet, though the painting actually precedes the series of marines which the French artist began in 1865 when he and Whistler visited the coast together.

The choice of the breaking wave motif and the quality of the paint itself—rough, impetuous strokes of thick paint, with the texture of the canvas frequently breaking through and making the impasto rougher still—suggests Courbet's influence. But within the idiom of "realism," Whistler was working gradually toward a style which was ultimately to abandon "that damned realism."

The Blue Wave: Biarritz is particularly interesting because the artist was obviously in mid-passage: two rival concepts of painting were at war within him and within the painting itself.

The rocks do have weight and solidity, but they are actually rendered as patches of broken color, with scarcely any distinction between horizontal and vertical planes, or planes of light and shadow. The rough handling of the paint suggests the texture of the rocks, but their forms are quite flat. The painter has abandoned the linear touches that defined edges and implied shadow planes in *The Coast of Brittany* (Plate 1).

Even in the wave which serves as the picture's focal point, the artist was fighting the tendency to grade color methodically from light to dark—the logical way to convey the deep inward curve of the form. Traditional modeling from dark to light (waves are darkest at the peak of the curve) appears in the distant breakers, but the nearest wave carries only the slightest hint of modeling. The drama of rock and wave is essentially a drama of flat, roughly textured shapes.

The sky, too, suggests the future direction of Whistler's art. Here the artist was free to indulge in the wispy, evanescent strokes—each stroke spontaneous and distinct, yet each melting into the fabric of paint—which were to become the essence of his "handwriting."

Plate 3

THE BEACH AT SELSEY BILL
Oil on canvas
24"x18¾" (61x47.6 cm.)
About 1865
New Britain Museum of American Art,
New Britain, Connecticut

Just four years separate *The Beach at Selsey Bill* and *The Coast of Brittany* (Plate 1); yet, in these four years, Whistler evolved a radically new vision of pictorial space.

Both pictures show figures on the vacant sand of a beach, with a strip of sea and a strip of sky beyond. Both depict a world of deep space, reaching to the far horizon. Even the colors are similar: brown sand, a strip of orange-brown rock, dark blue sea, lighter blue sky broken by bits of cloud. But the differences are profound.

Once again, the horizon line is high—one third down from the top of the rectangle—but now the effect is to tip the landscape upward, toward us, like an adjustable drawing table swinging from horizontal to vertical. The beach becomes a massive, flat plane of color, faintly darkened by a cloud shadow. The unorthodox picture format—a vertical landscape—paradoxically deepens the space and increases the impact of the squarish, two dimensional patch of sand color.

The figures are not people at all—unlike the sleeping fisher girl, complete with regional costume, in *The Coast of Brittany* (Plate 1) —but simply notes of color, diagonally balanced against the thin strip of dark blue which represents the water. The distant rock formation is as flat and featureless as the sea: not a wave in the water, not a crack in the rock. They are just balanced notes of complementary color—blue against orange—deftly dividing the space. Above them, the sky consists entirely of streaks and dabs, entirely without modeling: the clouds have no light or shadow sides as in *The Coast of Brittany* (Plate 1) or *The Blue Wave: Biarritz* (Plate 2).

Here pictorial space becomes the flat surface of the rectangular canvas, and it becomes the artist's job to organize that space. As in the best of Whistler's mature works, the design is simple. The rectangle is boldly divided by two lines: the horizon, which slashes the picture into two stark rectangles; and an imaginary vertical line which drops from the single floating cloud (just off center in the sky), through the break in the horizon line where the sea ends and the cliff begins, to the standing figure in black.

The viewer is asked to respond to the boldness of these simple design decisions—to the division of the picture plane by extremely sparse pictorial elements, placed with great care.

Plate 4

NOCTURNE: THE SOLENT
Oil on canvas
19¾"x36" (50.2x91.5 cm.)
1866
Thomas Gilcrease Institute, Tulsa, Oklahoma

In painting and repainting his canvases, Whistler sought the minimum number of pictorial elements—even the minimum number of strokes—to convey his message. Although he acknowledged the influence of Japanese color woodcuts and Chinese porcelains, no one really knows how much Chinese and Japanese painting Whistler had seen. Yet his concept of picture making—as a search for the irreducible—was distinctly oriental.

In this early nocturne, the artist hangs an almost monochromatic composition from the horizon line, which is a nearly invisible color break between water and sky; the line barely thickens at the right to suggest a strip of land. Ships, horizon, and land are all concentrated in the upper half of the canvas. The three ships in the foreground literally dangle from the horizon like clothes drying on a line, while a fourth ship is faintly suggested above the horizon. The essence of the design is in the intervals between the ships, the balance between these shapes and the strip of land, and the unorthodox placement of these minimal forms in the barren rectangle.

Like *The Beach at Selsey Bill* (Plate 3), this canvas abandons the thick, crusty paint quality which Whistler had learned from Courbet. The paint is almost as fluid as watercolor and the only texture is the streakiness of the brushwork, the marks of the bristles. Yet the textures are never monotonous, but always animated by the gesture of the brush. In *The Beach at Selsey Bill* (Plate 3), the direction of the strokes clearly determines the sloping shape of the beach and the swell of the sand. In *Nocturne: The Solent*, the brushwork conveys the ripple of the water and its constantly shifting texture. This strange, washy, casual brushwork is far less random than it seems.

Whistler's obsession with the minimum number of decisive strokes—perhaps learned from the oriental masters—is most striking in the painting of the ships. One can almost count the number of strokes required to paint each ship. The lights and their reflections—on ships, shore, and water—are literally a dot and a dash.

Plate 5

NOCTURNE IN BLUE AND GOLD: VALPARAISO
Oil on canvas
29¾"x39" (75.6x99 cm.)
1866
Freer Gallery of Art, Smithsonian Institution, Washington, D.C.

Again the vertical format and extremely high horizon line are combined to flatten pictorial space by tipping land and sea upward, toward the viewer.

But even more important is the time of day. Why is night so necessary to Whistler's art? In the dim, silvery light of the moon, spatial relationships become ambiguous. Detail is suppressed and only the general outlines of things—the big shapes—remain. Ships cease to be ships, but become flat forms, blurred by the night. In the all-pervading darkness, the distinction between near and far is minimized. Ships, water, wharf, and coastline melt into the blue haze and become patches of color lying on the surface of the canvas.

At night, atmospheric and linear perspective become meaningless. Consider the wharf in the foreground. In the crisp light of day, this form would plunge diagonally back into the space beyond, emphasizing the distinction between near and far, dramatizing the gap between the wharf and the ships. And in daylight, atmospheric perspective would clearly divide the picture into three planes: the dark, sharply focused foreground of the wharf; the somewhat less detailed middle tone of the fleet, forming the middle ground; and the pale shore, devoid of detail, forming the traditional background plane.

But night permitted Whistler to obliterate these distinctions. In the darkness, the wharf is flattened and no longer juts back into deep space, but becomes a five sided rectilinear form on the picture plane, broken by the dark notes of the figures, who are no more detailed than the ships. Nor is the wharf any darker or more sharply focused than the fleet, which, in turn, barely emerges from the flat, abstract shape of the land.

Thus, Whistler's new vision was not an arbitrary attempt to redesign nature, but a fresh look at the visible world. He learned from his French contemporaries to look intently at the fleeting effects of light and color, then painted the decisive moment when nature redesigned itself.

Plate 6

VARIATIONS IN PINK AND GREY: CHELSEA
Oil on canvas
24⅝"x16" (62.7x40.5 cm.)
Signed with the butterfly
About 1871
Freer Gallery of Art, Smithsonian Institution, Washington, D.C.

The oriental influence is obvious, of course, in such details as ladies with parasols, sprigs of foliage, and Whistler's little butterfly symbol at the left edge.

But the painting is really an abstract experiment in which curious, spidery, disembodied forms strike out into space. It is the gestures of these forms and the intervals between them which fascinated Whistler: the way in which the horizontals and verticals are never quite horizontal or vertical, but always slightly askew, tilting into the picture space in unexpected ways. Note how the foreground swings one way, how the fence changes direction, how the distant shoreline tilts in a direction opposite to the angle of the foreground. The jagged shapes of the masts, with their furled sails, chop between the boats, which slide across the bare space of the water and head slightly downhill, a direction which is reversed by the far shore and the skiff with the bending figure.

Throughout, the gesture of the brush itself reinforces the gestures of the forms. The streaky paint quality—which the Victorian audience attributed to mere carelessness—gives the texture of each shape an internal direction. And the over-all streakiness of the brushwork unifies the total fabric of paint, much as the "comma brushstroke" of the impressionists creates a continuous, integrated surface.

As in *Nocturne in Blue and Gold: Valparaiso* (Plate 5), the color scheme appears to be essentially monochromatic. But the narrow color range actually encompasses a surprising variety of hues. Touches of pink, brown, green, yellow, orange, and even specs of vibrant red emerge from the bluish haze. Yet the bluish haze always dominates, infiltrating every element on the canvas and producing what Whistler called a "skin." It was this "skin" that fascinated him in the work of Dutch masters like Terborch, Vermeer, De Hoogh—whose colors always seemed to lie beneath an almost invisible membrane of gray or gray-gold, like the overcast skies so typical of the Low Countries.

Plate 7

NOCTURNE IN BLACK AND GOLD:
ENTRANCE TO SOUTHAMPTON WATER

Oil on canvas
20"x30" (50.9x76.3 cm.)
Signed with the butterfly
1872 or 1874
Art Institute of Chicago, Chicago, Illinois
Stickney Fund

Whistler claimed to dislike Turner "who alone has dared to do what no artist would ever be fool enough to attempt . . . paint nothing less than the sun." Yet this audacious composition is surprisingly like the late work of Turner (which Whistler probably had never seen): a pictorial design that revolves around a void in dead center. Turner used the sun as the fiery bullseye of the swirling void, but the more discrete Whistler used the moon; typically, he placed his bullseye not in the vortex of the void, but slightly off center.

This was the sort of painting that branded Whistler as a fool, a madman, or a prankster in the eyes of most nineteenth century gallery-goers. By their standard, the painting simply had no content, no subject.

But this was precisely the point of the painting: it was a picture of space. The viewer was expected to react to the minimal character of the design; to what was left out; to the great, haunting spaces which were divided and punctuated with such economy of means. It was not the blurred ships or the faint shoreline which were Whistler's "subject"; these were merely the artist's means of organizing space, just as the composer organizes time.

Actually, the organization of the painting follows an old compositional rule of thumb, used by painters for centuries. The painter draws an imaginary horizontal line across his canvas, one third of the way down; he then draws a second imaginary horizontal two thirds of the way down, thus dividing the canvas into three horizontal sections of equal size. He does exactly the same thing with two vertical lines, dividing the rectangle into three vertical strips of equal size. The result is a grid which divides the rectangle into nine smaller rectangles of equal dimensions. The rule of thumb says that either of the horizontal lines will make a good place for the horizon, as it does here. In the same way, either of the vertical lines will be a logical axis for the main pictorial elements; note the placement of the three ships beneath the moon, their masts aligning very neatly with an imaginary vertical axis. Finally, the painter knows that any spot where the imaginary lines intersect will make a good focal point— which is just where Whistler has put the moon.

The construction of a rectilinear compositional grid became a dominant concern in Whistler's work. Beneath the indistinct forms of the nocturnes lies precise pictorial geometry.

Plate 8

Nocturne: Blue and Silver, Battersea Reach
Oil on canvas
19⅝"x30⅛" (49.9x76.5 cm.)
1870s
Freer Gallery of Art, Smithsonian Institution, Washington, D.C.

Whistler's concern with pictorial geometry is even more obvious in this stark composition of horizontals and verticals, relieved momentarily by diagonals.

Once again, the painter has established a grid system. Two strong horizontals—the far shore and the nearby barge—divide the canvas into thirds. An imaginary vertical, just off center, divides the rectangle in half; this center line is established by the end of the barge and a slender shape that juts upward from the distant shore, aligning precisely with the end of the barge. Two more verticals, the cluster of stacks on shore, and the mast on the barge, subdivide the canvas into quarters. Then a single diagonal establishes the focal point of the picture; the vertical mast in the foreground suddenly changes direction and the diagonal line breaks the strict pattern of horizontals and verticals. This change of pace is faintly echoed by two other masts to the right—each pitched at a slightly different angle—and the vague triangular rooftop on the shoreline to the left.

Described in this way, the entire design sounds coldly intellectual, more like a geometric exercise than a poem in paint. But the precision of the design is softened and enriched by Whistler's magical handling of paint. The edges of the forms melt into the moonlit sky and water. Inch by inch, these edges change, never hard, never completely lost, but constantly sharpening and blurring as if the light and atmosphere were shifting as you watch. Follow the upper edge of the shoreline, for instance, and observe how this fuzzy, but somehow precise contour keeps transforming itself as your eye moves across the canvas.

Whistler's contemporaries were not impressed. When a nocturne of Battersea Bridge was shown at the Ruskin trial, a baffled attorney asked: "Are those figures on top of the bridge intended for people?" Whistler said they were. "That is a barge beneath?" "I am very much flattered at your seeing that," the painter replied patiently. "The thing is intended simply as a representation of moonlight. My whole scheme was intended only to bring about a certain harmony of colour." Whistler's explanation seemed simple enough, but the pictures were so incomprehensible that one of them was quite soberly shown upside down. It was not a joke, but a genuine mistake; the court literally did not know which end was up.

Plate 9

NOCTURNE IN BLACK AND GOLD: THE FALLING ROCKET
Oil on wood panel
23¾"x18⅜" (60.3x46.6 cm.)
About 1874
Detroit Institute of Arts, Detroit, Michigan

"I have seen, and heard, much of Cockney impudence before now; but never expected to hear a coxcomb ask two hundred guineas for flinging a pot of paint in the public's face," wrote John Ruskin in *Fors Clavigera* when he saw this and a group of other Whistlers in the Grosvenor Gallery exhibit of 1877. *The Falling Rocket* became the most controversial of all Whistler's pictures when he sued the most powerful intellectual spokesman of the day for libel, won a farthing damages, and was forced into bankruptcy to pay legal costs.

To a nineteenth century viewer—trained to expect sharp edged detail, story telling content, recognizable people and places, and invisible brushwork—the painting must have seemed all daubs and spatters, like the first action paintings seemed in the twentieth century. Of course, it *is* all daubs and spatters (which are really flecks of color, knowingly placed with the tip of the brush) and this is precisely its charm. It is the spontaneous movement of the brush—scrubbing, smudging, dabbing, flicking—that gives the picture its vitality. The fireworks in Cremorne Gardens are merely an excuse for a dazzling display of painterly fireworks; the real subject of the picture is the pure delight of paint.

Although he used paint with abandon, Whistler never used color with abandon. Once again, an apparently monochromatic scheme envelopes a surprisingly wide range of colors. In the foreground are hints of brown, violet, mustard, russet, and orange. The rockets pick up these tones in vibrant, staccato notes, played against green as the eye ascends to the top of the picture. Throughout the painting, slight hints of warm color—brown and violet—peek through the dominant blue-black-green of the night sky.

Whistler was at the height of his powers when this picture was painted. Although the Ruskin trial had given him a historic opportunity to state the case for a new kind of painting, it was a Pyrrhic victory. His small following grew even smaller and many of his best pictures—like *The Falling Rocket*—remained unsold until the final decade of his life.

Plate 10

CHELSEA WHARF: GREY AND SILVER
Oil on canvas
24¼"x18⅟₁₆" (61.5x46 cm.)
About 1875
National Gallery of Art, Washington, D.C.
Widener Collection

Here is one of many variations of the theme explored in *Nocturne: Blue and Silver, Battersea Reach* (Plate 8). Now the grid of horizontals and verticals—with its diagonal center of interest—is contained within a vertical format.

Whistler consistently chose a narrow, virtually monochromatic color range for his nocturnes, knowing that the slightest break in this subtle scheme would have great impact. Thus, when "grey and silver" are suddenly interrupted by the warm tones of the rigging, these slight touches of muted brown and brown-gray sing out with unexpected power.

The artist's obsession with the decisive stroke—the one right stroke or series of strokes to interpret a particular form—is especially evident here. Note how the rigging is rendered with a combination of strokes, each retaining its individuality. One stroke may intersect with another, but each retains its identity; they are not ironed out with a soft hair blender (a favorite tool of the nineteenth century academician) to the textureless, enamel-like surface so popular with the contemporary audience.

The Pennells cite Arthur Severn's description of Whistler's method of painting a bridge. "He would look steadily at a pile for some time, then mix up the colour, then holding his brush quite at the end, with no mahlstick, make a downward stroke and the pile was done. I remember once his looking very carefully at a hansom cab that had pulled up for some purpose on the bridge, and in a few strokes he got the look of it perfectly."

He returned again and again to such simple subjects as these motionless barges along the shabby, industrial shoreline of the Thames. He was excited not only by their geometry, but by the possibility of finding design in the most unpromising subject matter.

"And when the evening mist clothes the riverside with poetry, as with a veil, and the poor buildings lose themselves in the dim sky, and the tall chimneys become companili, and the warehouses are palaces in the night, and the whole city hangs in the heavens, and fairly-land is before us—then the wayfarer hastens home; the working man and the cultured one, the wise man and the one of pleasure, cease to understand, as they have ceased to see, and Nature, who, for once, has sung in tune, sings her exquisite song to the artist alone, her son and master—her son in that he loves her, her master in that he knows her."

But to Whistler's contemporaries, a barge or a warehouse seemed a meager thing to paint when there was all of classical and modern literature to choose from for subject matter. If this perverse man was unwilling to paint people and bricabrac with invisible brushstrokes on large, smooth canvases, it must be sheer laziness or incompetence. Burne-Jones testified at the Ruskin trial: "Mr. Whistler gave infinite promise at first, but I do not think he has fulfilled it. I think he has evaded the great difficulty of painting, and has not tested his powers by carrying it out."

Plate 11

NOCTURNE: CREMORNE GARDENS, NO. 3
Oil on canvas
17⅝"x24¾" (44.9x63.1 cm.)
1875-1877
Freer Gallery of Art, Smithsonian Institution, Washington, D.C.

Nearly the entire canvas is a scrubby wash of color, animated by the texture of the canvas, which constantly breaks through the enveloping darkness. The paint was diluted to the consistency of watercolor, brushed on with casual, sweeping strokes, then partially scraped away to form the thinnest possible veil of tone, allowing the warp and woof of the canvas to strike through and create thousands of flecks of light that animate the night.

What emerges from this sea of shadow is nothing more than the slightly tilted rectangle of the portico caught in the moonlight, four roughly painted squares to indicate lighted windows, and four more blurs of light to suggest a second row of windows above. A diagonal reddish smear leads in from the left to balance the composition and lead the eye to two smudges—one dark, one light—are they figures? It is the most minimal design imaginable, no more than a flash of moonlight in the darkness.

Like Corot, Whistler was a master of warm and cool grays, those strangely colorful neutrals which are the stock in trade of the tonal painter, in contrast to the colorist. Within the obscurity of the night, Whistler found an astonishing range of greenish, brownish, yellowish, and bluish grays. Note how the "darkness" constantly changes color as the eye moves across the canvas. The color shifts are quite arbitrary, determined entirely by the need to keep the surface of the picture alive; Whistler would certainly not claim that he "saw" the night changing color before his eyes. And what could be more arbitrary than the decision to direct the viewer's attention by a series of ruddy streaks on which the entire composition hinges?

The technique of thinning oil paint to a wash, brushing it on, then scraping it away, was a masterful solution to the problem of painting the vibrant darkness which makes Whistler's nocturnes—and the best of his late, shadowy portraits—so memorable. But oil paint is not meant to be used that way. Radical dilution with turpentine or petrol wrecked the chemistry of the paint, while constant scraping slowly shaved away the fibers of Whistler's canvases until they were as fragile as old bedsheets. Sadly, many of Whistler's most interesting pictures have darkened badly and are too tender to repair.

Plate 12

TRAFALGAR SQUARE, CHELSEA
Oil on canvas
18⅝"x24⅝" (47.3x62.5 cm.)
1870s
Freer Gallery of Art, Smithsonian Institution, Washington, D.C.

Architectural subjects gave Whistler an opportunity to explore pictorial geometry in its purest form. With rare exceptions, he painted buildings head on, aligning walls and rooftops with the four edges of the canvas, much as the twentieth century architectural photographer visualizes his subject. When a form does recede into deep space—like the building on the right—it is flattened to become a tilted shape on the picture plane, rather than an architectural form in perspective.

Although Whistler avoided linear perspective—which uses receding lines to create the illusion of three dimensional space—he found that a touch of atmospheric perspective gave just the hint of three dimensionality that he sometimes needed. Thus, he might darken a few nearby forms ever so slightly and add the barest suggestion of detail, as he did here in the fence posts in the lower left hand corner. This not only places the buildings in their own shallow spatial plane, but creates a strong rectangle at the left to balance the looming building to the right.

Within this narrow range of tone and color—and within this strictly rectilinear setting—any slight deviation from the geometric becomes dramatic. Thus, the faintly darker notes and curling forms of the trees stand out like the famous little red caps of the fishermen in Corot's scores of gray-green landscapes. In the same way, tiny yellow squares of light (and a touch of red) are carefully placed among the buildings. The eye moves slowly along the horizontal center line of the picture, watching the subtle interplay of big, dark shapes (buildings); big, light shapes (sky); small, light shapes (windows); and the wandering lines of the trees and branches.

Plate 13

NOCTURNE IN GREY AND GOLD: CHELSEA SNOW
Oil on canvas
17½″x24″ (44.5x61 cm.)
'878
Fogg Art Museum, Harvard University, Cambridge, Massachusetts
Bequest of Grenville L. Winthrop

This appears to be the painting about which Whistler made his famous comment in "The Red Rag," published in *The World* in 1878: "My picture of a *Harmony in Grey and Gold* is an illustration of my meaning—a snow scene with a single black figure and a lighted tavern. I care nothing for the past, present, or future of the black figure, placed there because the black was wanted at that spot. All that I know is that my combination of grey and gold is the basis of my picture. Now this is precisely what my friends cannot grasp. They say, 'Why not call it "Trotty Veck," and sell it for a round harmony of golden guineas?'"

The Pennells say that "Whistler assured another of his friends that he had only to write 'Father, dear Father, come home with me now' on the painting for it to become the 'picture of the year.'"

Asked at the Ruskin trial for his definition of a nocturne, the artist explained: "I have perhaps, meant rather to indicate an artistic interest alone in the work, divesting the picture from any outside sort of interest which might have been otherwise attached to it. It is an arrangement of line, form, and colour first, and I make use of any incident of it which shall bring about a symmetrical result. Among my works are some night pieces; and I have chosen the word Nocturne because it generalises and simplifies the whole set of them."

He might have added that night, more than day, gave him the opportunity to experiment with patches of light and dark and color as disembodied shapes, functioning as abstract elements in a pictorial design. The night itself seemed to divest forms of their literary meaning by depriving them of detail. A pub ceased to be a pub and became a pattern of luminous rectangles, broken by streaks and patches of darkness. The snow and sky were no longer snow and sky, but luminous space, like the sky and water in his Thames nocturnes.

Whistler's painting, like the Japanese art he admired, is an art of interval. Space has an intense reality and it is the spaces between things that often determine the power of the composition. In *Nocturne in Grey and Gold: Chelsea Snow*, Whistler divides the canvas into three areas of ambiguous space: snow, sky, and the fused form of the dark buildings and trees. Snow and darkness are bridged by the tiny shape of the anonymous figure who steps from the blue-violet light to the obscurity beyond. Floating in the darkness are small notes of light—streaks, squares, dabs—whose apparently random placement turns the night into an abstract drama of intervals.

Plate 15

Nocturne in Blue and Silver: Battersea Reach
Oil on canvas
15½"x24¾" (39x63 cm.)
Signed with the butterfly
1870s
Isabella Stewart Gardner Museum, Boston, Massachusetts

Whistler said that his paintings were "the complete results of harmonies obtained by employing the infinite tones and variations of a limited number of colours." In the short-lived art school which he started in his later years, he emphasized the value of the limited palette. Frederick MacMonnies, who taught sculpture there, quoted Whistler: "My idea is to give them three or four colours—let them learn to paint the form and line first until they are strong enough to use the others. If they become so, well and good; if not, let them sink out of sight."

Whistler's own palette was limited and subdued. His yellows and browns were all earth colors—yellow ochre, raw sienna, Venetian red, Indian red, burnt sienna, umber—except for one brilliant color, vermilion, which he used only for accents. Black and white were essential, of course, for the tonal control he sought; these, with cobalt blue and mineral blue, dominated his nocturnes, where warm colors rarely appeared except to modify or accent the cool ones.

It was these pictures in particular that appealed to the French literary *avant-garde*. Laver points out that "Whistler's art, which had drifted so far away from the main current of French painting, was for many reasons particularly likely to appeal to the *littérateurs* of the *Symboliste* movement. They were tired of crude colours and fond of twilight. So was Whistler. Their taste was perfect, but lacking all robustness. So was his. They delighted in the suggestion of mystery, in contours lost in shadow, in figures that emerged from a misty background like the people of a dream. Whistler's later portraits satisfied all these requirements. Sometimes, a whole school of literature seems to possess a definite colour, and the colour of *Symbolisme* is grey-blue, just such a shade as Whistler mixed upon his palette when he sat down to paint a nocturne."

But Whistler's preference for blue-gray was more than a matter of taste. In contrast with hot colors like red and orange, which seem to advance toward the viewer, blue is a cool color and seems to recede, to draw away from the viewer. Thus, Whistler's nocturnes demand a new kind of effort from the audience. If the picture recedes from us, we must allow ourselves to be drawn in, we must move into the blue-gray haze and allow ourselves to be enveloped by it. He was asking the nineteenth century audience to experience art in a new way—to experience a painting by stepping inside it.

Plate 16

NOCTURNE: WESTMINSTER PALACE
Oil on canvas
18½"x24½" (47x62.3 cm.)
1870s
John G. Johnson Collection, Philadelphia, Pennsylvania

Whistler's search for the irreducible nocturne led—perhaps inevitably—to a composition which was pared down to just three bands of color, representing water, land, and sky. It was the most abstract possible statement of the theme, and the barest. For Whistler saw himself as the plainest of painters, a tight-lipped puritan who never "gossiped in paint," never said more than he had to say to get his point across. Although most of his contemporaries saw him as a trickster in search of bizarre effects, he hated the cleverness and the ostentatious brush-slinging of the virtuoso painter: "In my pictures there is no cleverness, no brush marks, nothing to astonish and bewilder, but simply a gradual, more perfect growth of beauty. It is this beauty my canvases reveal, not the way it is obtained."

To the French and English art public, "the Nocturnes looked so simple . . . that they seemed unfinished—just knocked off," wrote the Pennells. "No one knew the hard work that produced the simplicity. In no other paintings was Whistler as successful in following his own precepts and concealing traces of toil. One touch less and nothing would be left; one touch more and the spell would be broken, and night stripped of mystery."

The novelist and critic, George Moore, a sometime friend of the painter, was one of the few who recognized the boldness of Whistler's simplicity. *Nocturne: Westminster Palace* may have been the picture he was describing in *Modern Painting*, published in 1893: "Mr. Whistler's nights are the blue transparent darkness which are half of the world's life. Sometimes he foregoes even the aid of earthly light, and his picture is but luminous blue shadow, delicately graduated, as in the nocturne in M. Duret's collection—purple above and below, a shadow in the middle of the picture—a little less and there would be nothing."

In its present condition, the pervading color of the nocturne is not purple, but Whistler's familiar blue-green. If Moore was talking about the same canvas, it is impossible to know whether his description is at fault or the color has changed—which happened all too often with Whistler's unfortunate color chemistry.

Plate 17

THE LAGOON, VENICE:
NOCTURNE IN BLUE AND SILVER
Oil on canvas
20″x26″ (51x66 cm.)
About 1880
Museum of Fine Arts, Boston, Massachusetts
Emily L. Ainsley Fund

The monochrome of Whistler's nocturnes is constantly enlivened by hints of other colors, touches of warmth constantly breaking through the generally cool tonality. Walter Greaves, who assisted the painter during the period when the nocturnes were painted, told the Pennells that Whistler often prepared his canvases and panels—as the Venetian masters had done—with a tone that would contrast with the overlying colors.

"For the blue nocturnes, the canvas was covered with a red ground, or the panel was of mahogany . . . the red forcing up the blues laid on it. Others were done on a warm black . . ."

At other times, Whistler would prepare a ground that roughly approximated—rather than contrasted with—the final color. He would explain that "the sky is grey, and the water is grey, and, therefore, the canvas must be grey."

The spontaneity of the final painting was the result of meticulous planning. The underlying color of the canvas was prepared as one chooses a sheet of pastel paper, knowing that the tone of the surface would influence every stroke. The right underlying color would not only unify the tonality of the painting, but would accelerate and simplify the very job of painting, making it possible to complete the picture "at one go." The canvas would be unified not only in color, but by the over-all spontaneity of execution.

The entire color scheme was planned on the palette before a brush was touched to the canvas. The Pennells record Greaves' description of the palette. "At the top . . . the pure colours were placed, though, more frequently, there were no pure colours at all. Large quantities of different tones of the prevailing colour in the picture to be painted were mixed, and so much of the medium was used that he called it 'sauce.'

"When Whistler had arranged his colour-scheme on the palette," the Pennells continue, "the canvas . . . was stood on an easel, but so much 'sauce' was used that frequently it had to be thrown flat on the floor to keep the whole thing from running off. He washed the liquid colour on, lightening and darkening the tones as he worked." Sickert reported that Whistler used big housepainters' brushes (a favorite of the action painters in our century), rather than conventional artists' brushes, for the large sweeps of color.

The artist's concern with a unified surface even extended to his method of drying the finished picture. A neighbor in Chelsea remembered "seeing the Nocturnes set out along the garden wall to bake in the sun." Whistler experimented with drying times and temperatures by leaving some canvases indoors to dry slowly, while others were set outdoors to dry quickly. He was rumored to have left paintings outdoors in all kinds of weather: "It takes the gloss off them," he said, "that objectionable gloss which puts one in mind of a painfully new hat."

Plate 18

THE ANGRY SEA
Oil on wood panel
4⅞″x8½″ (12.4x21.7 cm.)
Reproduced actual size
Signed with the butterfly
Not later than 1884
Freer Gallery of Art, Smithsonian Institution, Washington, D.C.

In the 1880s, with the best of his portraits and nocturnes behind him, Whistler entered a new phase. Although he did not give up night pictures entirely, he seemed to rediscover the crisp light of day. He no longer relied on darkness to abstract and simplify nature for him. For the first time, he began to paint on location—most often at the seashore—in the open air, where shapes were sharply defined by the sunlight. The soft edges of the nocturnes gave way to the harder edges revealed by daylight. The muted tones of the night gave way to the stronger colors and broader color range of the day.

The tightly programmed spontaneity of his studio paintings gave way to genuine playfulness, to the kind of spontaneity which is forced upon the painter as he walks on the beach, never knowing what he will paint until he finds it. Whistler's simple means became simpler still as he sat in a bobbing boat—the boatmen struggling to hold it steady—trying to catch the form and gesture of a breaking wave in a few solid strokes.

He abandoned the mystery of the nocturnes for the most forthright painting he had ever done—paintings that communicate a direct and immediate response to nature that he never achieved in his studio pictures. He walked with his studio literally in his hand: a tiny "thumb box" of colors and brushes, and wood panels small enough to slip into an overcoat pocket. Relaxed and mobile, he could take his studio wherever impulse might lead—and the small panels of the 1880s and 1890s convey the kind of freshness and enthusiasm that we enjoy in Constable's oil sketches.

Whistler had once been accused of dashing off his painstaking studio pictures. Now he really *did* dash them off. But what emerged were not casual field sketches, but the most severely organized, most audaciously simplified paintings of his career. *The Angry Sea* is not much more than a series of horizontal strips of color, painted with sure, fluid strokes that are laid one next to the other, never softened, never blended. Each whitecap is a single stroke, and the slight irregularity of these strokes barely deviates from the strict horizontal design. The color is applied flatly and so thinly that the tone and texture of the wood panel strike through. Here Whistler's ideal of plain painting reached its ultimate expression.

Plate 19

A Note in Blue and Opal: The Sun Cloud

Oil on wood panel
4⅞″x8½″ (12.4x21.7 cm.)
Reproduced actual size
Not later than 1884
Freer Gallery of Art, Smithsonian Institution, Washington, D.C.

Like a character in a Restoration drama, Whistler hated the country: "There are too many trees in the country." This was not rhetoric, the kind of barb that Whistler enjoyed throwing at English gentry. His experiments in pictorial design were strongly tied to nature: he did not invent his compositions, but found them (like a true protegé of Courbet) in the visible world. Winding roads, rolling hills, and sporadic clusters of trees did not organize themselves into the pure—perhaps the word should be puritanical—geometry which he found in the city and at the seashore.

He preferred the bare design of the shore above all—"no great, full-blown, shapeless trees"—and even his rare views of the countryside are most often patterns of horizontals. In *A Note in Blue and Opal: The Sun Cloud*, the low horizon flattens the shape of the land into a horizontal strip. There *are* trees, but these, too, are subdued to linear geometry: one row of trees becomes a diagonal band that divides the foreground; others soften the horizon line, but are subdued by it.

The houses, as well, break the horizon line, but never break *away* from it. They are painted flatly, as rectilinear shapes.

The geometry of the landscape serves as a foil for the free forms of the clouds, which tilt and fly across the upper two thirds of the picture space. Although the clouds are ragged, Whistler has visualized them as flat forms on parallel axes, like clothes hanging out to dry on parallel clotheslines. The axes of the clouds tilt down as the landscape tilts upward.

Plate 20

GREY AND SILVER: THE LIFE BOAT
Oil on wood panel
4¹³⁄₁₆″x8½″ (12.3x21.6 cm.)
Reproduced actual size
Signed with the butterfly
Not later than 1884
Freer Gallery of Art, Smithsonian Institution, Washington, D.C.

Although Whistler greatly enriched his palette in these final years, he remained a master of grays. Here he returned to the color strategy of *Chelsea Wharf: Grey and Silver* (Plate 10); again, luminous warm and cool grays are suddenly heightened by touches of brown and a few strokes of orange are placed against the blue-gray of the boat.

There is the same quiet counterpoint in the brush strokes. Almost the entire picture is painted in long, lazy horizontal strokes, many of which carry completely across the width of the panel. The slightest variations in the character of the strokes—changes in width, density, pressure, or the speed of the hand—transform these smears and scrubs into waves, ripples, nearby shore, or distant land and clouds. Then, quite suddenly, the brush flicks in a few staccato strokes, a few vertical accents in a picture made of horizontals, which become figures or a mast breaking the horizon line.

Laver speculates about Whistler's extraordinary ability to create the illusion of color by using so *little* color. "It has been suggested that he was so sensitive to colour that he really thought he was painting scarlet when he was really painting pale pink, and that his browns and greys had for him an intensity which the normal eye failed to see. The explanation is a trifle fantastic, although it might serve to explain his love of twilight. Perhaps it is not unkind to suggest that he painted in low tones because low tones were very much easier to harmonize. The shrill concert of the early Italians, the full trumpet notes of Rubens seem to have been beyond the capacity of nineteenth-century artists. The pre-Raphaelites left the harmony to look after itself: Whistler cut out everything in the orchestra but the woodwind."

Plate 22

NOCTURNE: GRAND CANAL, AMSTERDAM
Watercolor on paper
6¹⁵⁄₁₆″x11³⁄₁₆″ (22.7x28.4 cm.)
Signed with the butterfly
Not later than 1884
Freer Gallery of Art, Smithsonian Institution, Washington, D.C.

Whistler's new freedom led him, quite naturally, into watercolor. He had painted sporadically in this medium, but generally in a conventional technique. Now his new interest in the casual, the unpredictable, the accidental, led him to take a new look at this most perverse of all painting media. For watercolor, more than any other medium, has a tendency to go its own way and leave the painter behind, like a horse who throws its rider and gallops off. The watercolorist *must* be like the horseman who enjoys riding an untamed—and fundamentally untamable—animal, fighting to maintain *some* control, but always prepared to go where circumstance may carry him.

In *Nocturne: Grand Canal, Amsterdam*, the artist purposely chose the most unpredictable of all watercolor techniques: the so-called wet paper method. The rough sheet of paper is first soaked or covered with clear water. Into this sea of moisture, the colors are floated and immediately begin to spread and blur in all directions. Edges quickly disappear and shapes became indistinct as the color moves over the sheet according to its own unpredictable laws. The artist must race to control his medium, putting dabs of color where they are needed, wiping color away if it goes where it is not wanted, exploiting "happy accidents" and washing away unhappy ones before the paper dries and the painting is irrevocable.

The method fails more often than it succeeds and is always a gamble. When it does succeed, the picture conveys the excitement of the artist's struggle with the medium.

Here Whistler has returned to the limited color scheme of the nocturnes, perhaps because he felt that controlling watercolor on wet paper would be enough of a problem without attempting to control a complex color scheme. The drama of the painting grows out of the flickering pattern of lighted windows and reflections in the water—most of them blurred, some of them hard edged—and the washy shapes that barely emerge from the darkness. The random, accidental quality of the spots of color is held in control by the simple, geometric composition, which divides the picture into roughly parallel bands, almost horizontal, but not quite.

Plate 23

LOW TIDE
Oil on wood panel
5⅜″x9¼″ (13.8x23.5 cm.)
Reproduced actual size
Signed with the butterfly
1880s or 1890s
Freer Gallery of Art, Smithsonian Institution, Washington, D.C.

Inez Bate, who became Whistler's assistant during his brief period of teaching at the Académie Carmen (named for his model), quoted her mentor's views on composition in his final years: "The faculty for composition is part of the artist, he has it, or he has it not—he cannot acquire it by study—he will only learn to adjust the composition of others, and, at the same time, he uses his faculty in every figure he draws, every line he makes, while in the large sense, composition may be dormant from childhood until maturity, and there it will be found in all its fresh vigour, waiting for the craftsman to use the mysterious quality in his adjustment of his perfect drawings to fit their spaces."

No one can say whether he would have agreed with these words two decades earlier, when he was working so slowly and painfully to perfect his "arrangements," but he ultimately came to believe that there were no laws of composition, just intuitions. *Low Tide* suggests the most intuitive approach to pictorial design, with its jumble of boats and shacks in the upper half of the panel, chopped off by the upper edge of the frame, and its bare stretch of sand filling the entire lower half of the rectangle. The boats and shacks, like the beach, are really not much more than patches of color and tone, knowingly placed side by side. Why this arbitrary, seemingly accidental design works at all defies analysis, but it does. The grid systems and pictorial geometry of the nocturnes have disappeared; the aging painter has at last felt free to abandon planning for pure instinct.

Whistler had never been prodigal with paint or with brush strokes; he seemed to regard paint as a necessary evil, to be used as sparingly as possible, though one could not paint pictures without it. Now his means became even simpler; even less paint on the surface, even fewer strokes, and no attempt to conceal the artist's sometimes erratic handwriting. To be free and instinctive meant to be forthright, transparent, unassuming. "Be quite simple," he told his students, "no fussy foolishness, you know, and don't try to be what they call strong. When a picture smells of paint, it's what they call strong."

More than ever, he valued the innocent eye. Confronted by three new pupils, he asked each where he had studied. "With Chase," said one. "Couldn't have done better," said Whistler. "With Bonnat," said the next. "You couldn't have done better." "I have never studied anywhere, Mr. Whistler," said the third. "I am sure you could not have done better," said the old man.

His health failing and the end in sight, Whistler had rediscovered his own innocence in these last spontaneous paintings. He knew that he had achieved a breakthrough when he wrote to the Pennells in the late 1890s: "I could almost laugh at the extraordinary progress I am making and the lovely things I am inventing—work beyond anything I have ever done before."

Plate 24

CHELSEA SHOPS
Oil on wood panel
5¼"x9¼" (13.5x23.4 cm.)
Reproduced actual size
Signed with the butterfly
1880s or 1890s
Freer Gallery of Art, Smithsonian Institution, Washington, D.C.

In his wanderings through the streets of London, Whistler became fascinated with the geometry of shop fronts and painted many small panels which were essentially rectangles within rectangles, like *Nocturne in Brown and Gold: Chelsea Rags* (Plate 14). He looked at these architectural subjects head-on and factually recorded the pattern that he saw. (He hated the visionary architecture of Turner, who "must invent, imagine architecture as no architect could design it, and no builder who could set it up.")

In *Chelsea Shops*, Whistler pointedly avoided the traditional "rule" of variety in composition that states that the picture area should *never* be divided into sections of equal size and shape. Here, he purposely split the panel horizontally into two roughly equal rectangles; split the upper rectangle into four roughly equal boxes; further subdivided the shop fronts into upper and lower stories with second story windows of almost identical size and shape; and generally kept variety to a minimum. The only traces of variety are in the shapes of the ground floor shop fronts, where the placement and size of doors, windows, awnings, and tiny figures do change from one rectangle to the next. But the only real "action" appears in the faint tilt of the road and the figure laboring uphill in dead center.

Of course, it is color and tone that provide the variety that is lacking in the spatial organization. In these small architectural panels, Whistler clearly anticipated twentieth century geometric abstraction —particularly those painters who rely upon dynamic color within a static geometric scheme.

In his teaching, Whistler insisted on a complete color plan before the student touched the canvas. Inez Bate explained that the entire color scheme of the painting was mixed on the palette: "Many brushes were used, each one containing a full quantity of every dominant note, so that when the palette presented as near a reproduction of the model and background as the worker could obtain, the colour could be put down with a generous flowing brush.

"Mr. Whistler would often refrain from looking at the students' canvas, but would carefully examine the palette, saying that there he could see the progress being made, and that it was really much more important for it to present a beautiful appearance, than for the canvas to be fine and the palette inharmonious. He said, 'If you cannot manage your palette, how are you going to manage your canvas?' "

Such precision of color is obvious in *Chelsea Shops*, where rectangles of yellow, brown, gray, olive and off-white are carefully locked together, then highlighted here and there with tiny notes of red, blue, and white. With characteristic restraint, Whistler has decided that either the colors or the shapes must dance—but not both—and he has chosen in favor of the colors.

Plate 25

THE BUTCHER'S SHOP
Oil on wood panel
4¹⁵⁄₁₆"x8⁹⁄₁₆" (12.5x21.8 cm.)
Reproduced actual size
Signed with the butterfly
1880s or 1890s
Freer Gallery of Art, Smithsonian Institution, Washington, D.C.

"It is Mr. Whistler's way to choose people and things for painting which other painters would turn from, and to combine these oddly chosen materials as no other painter would choose to combine them," wrote one of the artist's early detractors in the *London Times*. The critic was right, of course, for who but Whistler (and Rembrandt and Daumier) would have chosen to find beauty in a store front filled with bloody sides of beef?

Again the view is head-on and the shop front becomes a rectangle, with rectangular patches of color at either side, faintly indicating adjacent doorways or windows. Within the dark square of the butcher shop, the hanging forms of the beef are non-rectangular shapes; but they are flat and symmetrical, suggesting rectangles with symmetrical slices taken out of them.

The Butcher's Shop is a particularly interesting example of Whistler's use of neutrals—grays and browns—to provide a subdued setting for one strong color, which appears, by contrast, to be more intense than it actually is. Inez Bate remembered that Whistler taught his students that the subject "should be presented in a simple manner, without an attempt to obtain a thousand changes of colour that there are in reality. . ." He urged the student to resist the temptation to "present a brightly coloured image, pleasing to the eye, but without solidity and non-existent on any real plane."

Miss Bate noted that Whistler constantly stressed that the visible world was much lower in tone than artists normally painted it, ". . . that long accustoming oneself to seeing crude notes in Nature, spots of red, blue, and yellow in flesh where they are not, had harmed the eye, and the training to readjust the real, quiet, subtle note of Nature required long and patient study." Miss Bate quoted a characteristic epigram: "To find the true note is the difficulty; it is comparatively easy to employ it when found."

Long after his work had lost every trace of the Courbet influence, Whistler was still rooted in realism, still committed to observation: "one *fact* is worth a thousand misty imaginings."

Plate 26

GREEN AND GOLD: THE GREAT SEA
Oil on wood panel
5⅜"x9¼" (13.8x23.5 cm.)
Reproduced actual size
Signed with the butterfly
1880s or 1890s
Freer Gallery of Art, Smithsonian Institution, Washington, D.C.

Painters often have favorite designs: Turner's vortex, Chardin's single looming form surrounded by subsidiary forms, Rubens' spiral, Watteau's landscape split vertically by a void, the L shape of the Barbizon painters, the Renaissance pyramid. They explore these compositional ideas again and again, restating and reexamining them, discovering an astonishing number of new possibilities in a basically simple concept. It is often surprising how few design ideas a great painter actually has; his greatness often consists in his ability to find endless subtle variations within this limited compositional range.

Having arrived at the irreducible statement of land, water, and sky as three parallel bands—first tried in such paintings of the 1870s as *Nocturne: Westminster Palace* (Plate 16)—Whistler persistently returned to this theme, painting variation after variation. In the small marines of the 1880s and 1890s, he became more obsessed with this minimal design than ever before; there are literally dozens of reexaminations of this concept.

He tried raising the horizon line and boldly leaving half the picture bare sand, as in *The Angry Sea* (Plate 18). Here, in *Green and Gold: The Great Sea,* he dropped the horizon line below the center of the rectangle, opening a massive space of sky to the free play of the brush.

Winslow Homer, a taciturn New Englander who was America's greatest painter of the sea, had said, "It takes only two waves to make a seascape." It is interesting to note how little sea there is in Whistler's marine paintings. The water frequently occupies only a thin strip of green and white in a composition which is nearly all sand and sky. Yet these few strokes convey the full power of breakers rolling in from the limitless ocean. And this is just the secret of these tiny panels: *accentuated* by the bare beach and the spacious sky, the thunder of the waves is concentrated in a single dark band, broken by bars of and clots of white, painted with vigor and intensity.

Plate 27

LONDON BRIDGE
Watercolor on paper
6⅞"x10¹⁵⁄₁₆" (17.5x27.8 cm.)
1880s or 1890s
Freer Gallery of Art, Smithsonian Institution, Washington, D.C.

Here Whistler's favorite design concept of three parallel bands appears in still another variation. The bridge splits the paper and creates roughly equal areas of water and sky. As he did in most of the seascapes, Whistler concentrated nearly all activity in the center strip—the bridge—leaving water and sky virtually bare, except for the deftly placed puff of smoke that ascends from the focal point of the composition.

The activity within the center strip is again a restrained drama of intervals and shapes within shapes. To begin with, the bridge is not a rigid horizontal, but a flattened arc. Within this arc, a series of other arcs appear: the arches which echo the form of the bridge. The center of interest is the cluster of river craft—flagged by the puff of smoke—the orange boat placed at the meeting point of the left hand arch and the middle arch, the black barge moving across the middle arch, which is subdivided by two vertical stacks. Having established the repetitive rhythm of the arc shaped bridge and the three arches within it, Whistler then focused the viewer's attention by breaking the rhythm at the picture's focal point.

The artist's command of the viewer's attention is strengthened by what photographers call "selective focus." Most of *London Bridge* is a variation of the wet paper method—like *Nocturne: Grand Canal, Amsterdam* (Plate 22)—in which touches of color simply wash into one another and coalesce into a lively blur. Only along the bridge is this blur interrupted by any sharply defined detail. Out of the haze appear a fragment of a building, a few masts, some lines to define the bridge, a few carriages crossing the bridge, and the harbor craft themselves. But even these slight details go in and out of focus, dissolving momentarily into the fluid color that covers most of the paper. Look at the black barge in the center: the stern is sharply defined, hard edged, but the bow and the water line are soft edged, fuzzy, melting into the surrounding wash of wet color.

Whistler did not really expect such paintings to be understood, "There is mystery here," he said, but "the people don't want it. What they like is when the east wind blows, when you can look across the river and count the wires in the canary bird's cage on the other side."

Plate 28

THE WHITE HOUSE
Oil on wood panel
5⅜"x9¼" (13.6x23.6 cm.)
Reproduced actual size
1880s or 1890s
Freer Gallery of Art, Smithsonian Institution, Washington, D.C.

The fluidity of watercolor gave Whistler the sense of controlled spontaneity he had sought in his work from the very beginning. He had always defied the inherent nature of oil paint—inherently a slower moving, buttery medium—by thinning it to what he called a "sauce." Now, in his final years, many of Whistler's small oils really began to look like watercolors.

Among watercolorists, one of the rules of thumb is that the painting surface—usually sparkling white paper—should be allowed to shine through the transparent color. In fact, watercolorists often avoid covering the sheet completely, but allow spots of bare paper to appear between color areas, or even within color areas; these flecks of light add vitality to the surface.

In his late oils, Whistler frequently adopted a similar approach. Washy strokes of water-thin oil paint were casually streaked across the panel, allowing the often conflicting texture of the wood to break through the color and appear between the strokes. The grain of the panel would act as a subtle counterpoint to the gesture of the brush. In *The White House*, the panel has been primed with a pale gray, which still does not conceal the texture of the wood. There are still other oils of that period in which Whistler has actually painted on the bare wood, whose rippling grain winds through the color.

Having once said that the painting should conceal all traces of the work that went into it, Whistler now let the viewer see everything —every trace of the artist's moving hand, every casual impulse registered in paint, even the naked surface on which the picture was painted. The viewer was to participate in the process of painting, to feel that he was looking over the artist's shoulder. The painting became an X-ray of itself, a totally transparent record of the act of creation.

Plate 29

THE SEA AND SAND
Oil on wood panel
5¼"x9¼" (13.4x23.4 cm.)
Reproduced actual size
Signed with the butterfly
1880s or 1890s
Freer Gallery of Art, Smithsonian Institution, Washington, D.C.

When success arrived at last in the 1880s and 1890s, Whistler was bitter about the fact that the public seemed to care most about the pictures of the 1860s and 1870s.

"He was furious with the critic who stated that his medal was awarded for *The Little White Girl*," said the Pennells. "The statement was offensive because, he said, 'the critics are always passing over recent work for early masterpieces, though all are masterpieces; there is no better, no worse; the work has always gone on, it has grown, not changed, and the pictures I am painting now are full of qualities they cannot understand to-day any better than they understood *The Little White Girl* at the time it was painted."

Although Whistler surely overstated the case (as usual) when he insisted that "all are masterpieces," he had lived with a studio full of unsold pictures long enough to be aware of the continuity of his work. More important, he saw the steady growth which had led, at last, to the small, unassuming panels and watercolors which were actually the culmination of his life's work.

It is revealing to compare *Alone with the Tide* (Plate 1), *The Beach at Selsey Bill* (Plate 3), and *The Sea and Sand*, to see how a single theme has been restated, refined, and abstracted at three critical points in the artist's career. All three show figures on a long stretch of beach with a strip of sea in the distance. Each is a successful painting in itself. But over the years, flat shapes become flatter, space becomes more and more dominant, the artist's handwriting becomes freer and more spontaneous, a sparse pictorial design becomes sparser still.

Particularly fascinating is the steady reduction of the artist's means: each picture seems to contain less paint and fewer strokes per square inch. The marine painter's temptation is to pile on the paint with great gusto to match the vigor of the subject. But Whistler's strategy was to use only enough paint and energy to catch the decisive moment. The Pennells report his method: "When the wave broke and the surf made a beautiful line of white, he painted this at once, then all that completed the beauty of the breaking wave, then the boat passing, and then, having got the movement and the beauty that goes almost as soon as it comes, he put in the shore or the horizon."

Plate 30

BLUE AND SILVER: CHOPPING CHANNEL
Watercolor on paper
5½"x9½" (14.1x24.2 cm.)
Reproduced actual size
Signed with the butterfly
1880s or 1890s
Freer Gallery of Art, Smithsonian Institution, Washington, D.C.

In the 1860s and 1870s, when Whistler was working hardest on the design of his nocturnes, his critics charged that his paintings had no composition. In the 1880s and the 1890s, when he had reduced the design of many of his best pictures to a division of the space into mere horizontals, his detractors were, in a sense, right.

In this watercolor, Whistler has done nothing more than divide the picture space into two rectangular zones for sea and sky, each animated by the artist's handwriting. The sea is a pattern of violent brushwork, the gesture of the brush matching the gesture of the wave; the waves churn together, bleak, unbroken by a majestic line of foam or a sail that would "compose" the picture, create a center of interest, and shatter the effect of fierce monotony. The sky, too, is simply a pattern of alternating areas of light and dark gray— gray clouds scuddling through a barren sky in rhythm with the sea. The threatening atmosphere of the painting is the sum of color and brushwork, strengthened by the decision that the right design is no design at all.

Whistler knew that small scale was a source of power. Visions like *Blue and Silver: Chopping Channel* gained intensity by being compressed into a space no larger than most of his etchings. Within this tiny rectangle, every stroke counted and there was simply no room for the extraneous stroke. He explained his stand in a famous set of "Propositions" on the art of etching:

I. That in Art, it is criminal to go beyond the means used in its exercise.

II. That the space to be covered should always be in proper relation to the means used for covering it.

III. That in etching, the means used, or instrument employed, being the finest possible point, the space to be covered should be small in proportion.

IV. That all attempts to overstep the limits insisted upon by such proportion, are inartistic thoroughly, and tend to reveal the paucity of the means used . . .

Plate 31

NOCTURNE: OPAL AND SILVER
Oil on wood panel
8"x10⅛" (20.3x35.7 cm.)
Signed with the butterfly
1880s or 1890s
Freer Gallery of Art, Smithsonian Institution, Washington, D.C.

In his experiments with the division of the picture space into soft edged bands of color—see *Nocturne in Blue and Silver: Battersea Reach* (Plate 15) and *Nocturne: Westminster Palace* (Plate 16)—Whistler came steadily closer to abolishing the distinction between the three. Here, in *Nocturne: Opal and Silver*, the distant land is no more than a faint darkening of the over-all haze, just above the midpoint of the rectangle. A few almost invisible strokes suggest the arc of the bridge. Two dark river craft send the reflections of their lights stabbing downward into the water. A third light appears above the bridge (is it a tower on the far shore or is it the bridge itself?) sending a long reflection downward between the boats.

The mysterious, yet strangely convincing sense of space and atmosphere is enhanced by the texture of the paint itself. Although the entire panel is a pale gray, the darkest tones are concentrated in the lower part of the painting, where the brushwork is boldest and roughest. As the eye moves upward, the ragged brush strokes melt away into the haze, which gradually lightens to suggest some faint light emanating from the overcast sky. This delicate shift in tone and paint quality is just enough to indicate foreground and distance.

Rodin, the great sculptor of light and atmosphere, recognized the strength that underlay the seeming evanescence of Whistler's art. "Whistler was a painter whose drawing had great depth . . . . His feeling for form was not only that of a good painter, it was that of a sculptor. He had an extraordinary delicacy of sentiment, which made some people think that his basis was not very strong, whereas it was, on the contrary, both strong and firm.

"He understood atmosphere most admirably," Rodin continued, describing one of the Thames views as "a marvel of depth and space. The landscape itself is nothing; there is merely this great extent of atmosphere, rendered with consummate art.

"Whistler's art will lose nothing by the lapse of time; it will gain; for one of its qualities is energy, another is delicacy; but the greatest of all is its mastery of drawing."

The emphasis on Whistler's mastery of drawing seems strange at first glance, for his paintings show very little evidence of "draftsmanship" as we normally define it; nor are Whistler's drawings his best work. More surprising still is Rodin's comparison of Whistler's two dimensional art with sculpture. But the French word for drawing is *dessin*, which also means design. And the sculptor's definition of drawing is not the ability to draw lines around things, but the ability to visualize forms in space—and space itself.

Whistler teachings confirmed Rodin's insight. The students "were taught to look upon the model as a sculptor would," Inez Bate told the Pennells, "using the paint as a modeller does his clay; to create on the canvas a statue, using the brush as a sculptor his chisel, following carefully each change of note, which means 'form' . . . and make it, first of all, *really and truly exist in its proper atmosphere . . .*" The conviction that form was inseparable from light and space was basic to Whistler's art, as it was to Rodin's.

Plate 32

THE SAD SEA: DIEPPE
Oil on wood panel
4¹⁵⁄₁₆″x8½″ (12.5x21.7 cm.)
Reproduced actual size
1880s or 1890s
Freer Gallery of Art, Smithsonian Institution, Washington, D.C.

Whistler's late seaside panels reached their ultimate simplicity—and audacity—in this composition. The sand is no more than a tilted rectangle of brown. Sea and sky merge into a second tilted rectangle of gray, edged with a ripple of foam where land and water meet. The barren design is broken only by a few dabs of black, brown, and white to suggest figures, three in dead center, four on the horizon. It is the barest possible statement. Speaking to his students, Whistler "pointed out that a child, in the simple innocence of infancy, painting the red coat of the toy soldier red indeed, is in reality nearer the great truth than the most accomplished trickster with his clever brushwork and brilliant manipulation of many colours."

His goal in these final paintings was to abandon all cleverness. "The modern painter has no respect for anything but his own cleverness, and he is sometimes so clever that his work is like that of a bad boy, and I'm not sure that he ought not to be taken out and whipped for it. Cleverness!—well, cleverness has nothing to do with art; there can be the same sort of cleverness in painting as that of the popular officer who cuts an orange into fancy shapes after dinner."

The tiny paintings of Whistler's last twenty years—so plain, so unassuming, yet so vital—were the product of a decision to abandon all show and work with the innocent eye of the child "painting the red coat of the toy soldier red." The very choice of a format so small that his pictures risked going unnoticed (in an era of big salon pieces) was a decision in favor of pure integrity. If these small panels and watercolors were to impress anyone at all, they would impress by the purity of the artist's vision and the transparency of his means.

The analogy of these last pictures with "imagism"—the radical movement which strove to restore simplicity and directness to English and American poetry—is hard to resist. For Ezra Pound, writing in 1912, saw Whistler as a posthumous comrade-in-arms in the campaign to clear the arts of literary pretensions and technical bravura. At the outset of the "imagist" crusade, Pound called Whistler "our own great artist, and even this informal salute . . . may not be out of place at the threshold of what I hope is an endeavour to carry into our American poetry the same sort of life and intensity which he infused into modern painting."

Edited by Susan E. Meyer
Design by James Craig
Composed in ten point Janson by Howard O. Bullard, Typographers
Printed in Japan by Toppan Printing Company, Ltd.